Wicked
SPRINGFIELD
MISSOURI

D1548139

Wicked SPRINGFIELD MISSOURI

THE SEAMY SIDE OF THE QUEEN CITY

LARRY WOOD

Charleston — London

THE
History
PRESS

Published by The History Press
Charleston, SC 29403
www.historypress.net

Copyright © 2012 by Larry Wood
All rights reserved

Back cover: Street scene of Springfield square, circa 1910.
Courtesy of Springfield–Greene County library.

First published 2012

Manufactured in the United States

ISBN 978.1.60949.735.4

Library of Congress CIP data applied for.

Contents

Introduction

In my introduction to *Wicked Joplin*, I mentioned that, when I was growing up in the Springfield area during the 1950s and 1960s, I occasionally heard old-timers comment on the wild reputation Joplin had in previous years. I never heard people talk about Springfield in the same vein, and from the time I became personally familiar with Springfield in the mid-1950s, it was always a pretty law-abiding town. At least, it seemed so to me.

As an author of Ozarks history, I have long known, of course, that Springfield during its early days was a rough-and-tumble frontier town that saw its share of violent events, like Wild Bill Hickok's gunfight on the public square. But the town just didn't seem to be enough of a mecca for sin and vice to be an apt subject for a whole book about the notorious side of its past. Even as I was writing *Wicked Joplin*, it never occurred to me that I might write a similar book about Springfield's history.

My opinion began to change when I started researching *Civil War Springfield*. It didn't surprise me that various kinds of vice existed in Springfield during the Civil War. After all, Springfield was a Union post during the war, and throughout history, wherever young, single men have congregated in large numbers, vice has been sure to follow. What did surprise me was how prevalent vice was and how many individuals continued to commit the crimes they had been charged for.

I was still not convinced, however, that such iniquity continued in Springfield after the war at a level that was sufficient to justify an entire book about it. Indeed, preliminary research supported my theory. Despite the fact that Springfield had its share of colorful characters who frequented the dens of Joplin during the 1870s and 1880s, the city itself never rivaled Joplin in terms of lawlessness during the latter part of the nineteenth century. What my later research has led me to believe, however, is that Springfield's comparatively tame reputation was due in part to the city's ability to hide or cover up most of its sins, unlike Joplin.

More to the point, the heyday of immorality in Springfield simply came later than it did in Joplin. While Joplin reached its zenith as a wild, wide-open town during the boom decades of the late 1800s, debauchery did not hold sway in Springfield until the early 1900s, after the Frisco passenger depot moved to Main Street and a hotel district flourished nearby. Some of the testimony in the grand jury books of Greene County describing the escapades and cavorts along College Street during the first two decades of the twentieth century would make even Joplinites blush. As Robert Neumann, director of the Greene County Records and Archives Center, suggested to me early on in my research for this book, maybe Springfieldians were just "slow learners." Like many slow learners, though, once the good folk of Springfield learned how to sin and carouse, they soon became masters of the discipline.

Acknowledgements

Much of my research for this book was conducted at the Greene County Archives and Records Center, and I want to thank director Robert Neumann and his staff for their help during the project. I especially want to thank Robert for being the first person to read the manuscript and for freely sharing his considerable knowledge of early Springfield. I would also like to thank Steve Haberman for helping me retrieve materials.

I also visited the local history section of the Springfield–Greene County Library several times during my research for this project, and I would like to thank Patti Hobbs, Michael Glenn, John Rutherford and Michael Price for their help during those visits.

In addition to serving as the primary facilities for my research, the Greene County Archives and Records Center and the Springfield–Greene County Library each supplied several illustrations for this book, and I want to thank them for that service as well.

I borrowed a number of Springfield newspapers on interlibrary loan during my research, and I want to thank Patty Crane, Jason Sullivan, Cheryl Smith, Chris Hamm and Jill Halbach-Boswell of the reference department of the Joplin Public Library for filling those orders for me.

Finally, I would like to thank my wife, Gigi, who has served as a proofreader for several of my previous books. This time, she took on the role of research assistant, and I thank her for performing that task and, more importantly, for her continued support.

Chapter One

The Frontier Years

In 1830, John P. Campbell settled near the present-day intersection of Jefferson and Water Streets. In 1835, he laid out Springfield and donated fifty acres to the town. That same year, Springfield was named the seat of Greene County, which had been formed two years earlier. In 1837, a courthouse was built on the square, and in 1838, the town was officially incorporated.

Springfield's growth was slow and steady at first; in fact, it took about twenty-five years for the town to achieve a population of roughly 1,300 people before the Civil War. Lacking telegraph service or a railroad, Springfield remained very much a frontier town during the prewar years. Serious crimes were rare, although those that did occur were noteworthy, and there was little sexual misconduct. Liquor and gambling, however, were prevalent almost from the town's founding. Fistfights and other forms of rowdiness were frequent occurrences as well, and liquor often played a part in these disturbances.

The very first murder in Springfield was an infamous case involving several of the leading citizens of Greene County. In the fall of 1836, John Roberts appeared before Greene County Court Judge Charles S. Yancey on a minor charge. Roberts, who owned a mill and a distillery just east of Springfield near present-day Highway 65, had served as the county's first coroner, but he had been involved in at least two serious affrays and was considered a rough character. In 1833, he had been charged with assault with intent to kill for stabbing Thomas Horn (who later became sheriff of Greene County). Although the criminal case was dropped the following year, Horn, with Yancey acting as his attorney, sued Roberts for trespass and assault. Then in 1835, Roberts went to trial on a new charge of assault with intent to kill after slitting the ear of Kindred Rose, but the jury failed to reach a verdict. When Roberts came before Judge Yancey in 1836, county clerk John P. Campbell, who had testified against Roberts in both assault cases, was also present. Roberts and Campbell started exchanging heated words, and Yancey told them to settle down. Campbell obeyed, but Roberts turned his ire toward the bench, reportedly telling the judge that he would say what he damn well pleased, in Yancey's court or any other. Yancey fined Roberts twenty dollars for the outburst. Roberts paid the fine but afterward began making threats against the judge and taunting him whenever he happened to see Yancey in public, especially if Roberts had been drinking, which was not an infrequent occurrence. (Roberts also filed a suit against Yancey, but it is not known whether the suit pertained to the fine Yancey had levied against him.) Yancey bore Roberts's insults for several months, walking away from confrontations on more than one occasion.

Then one day during the late summer of 1837, Roberts again appeared on the streets of Springfield. Learning that his old nemesis was in town, Yancey told lawyer Littleberry Hendricks that he would not let Roberts intimidate him again. Hendricks advised Yancey to go home in order to avoid another confrontation, and the two men started together toward the judge's house. Near the northwest corner of the square, however, they ran into Roberts, who again began taunting the judge. The two adversaries briefly exchanged words, and then Yancey told Roberts not to follow him any farther and started to walk away. As he turned, however, he noticed Roberts, who was known to carry a big knife, reach into his coat. Judge Yancey, thinking Roberts was going for the weapon, pulled out a pistol and shot him. He then pulled out a second pistol and was in the act of firing again when Hendricks knocked the weapon upward, sending the ball into the air. According to an account of this incident that appeared in the *Springfield Missouri Weekly Patriot* years later, Roberts shouted, "Don't shoot, I am a dead man now!" as he collapsed and died.

In 1838, Yancey was charged with manslaughter in Roberts's death. Even though Roberts was apparently reaching for his glasses case rather than his knife when he was killed, Yancey was found not guilty. Later, he was appointed a judge of the Greene County Circuit Court.

Another notorious killing occurred in Springfield close on the heels of the Yancey-Roberts case. One day in early 1838, several men were inside the grocery owned by R.J. McElhany eating, drinking and having a good time. (During the mid-1800s, a grocer often sold liquor as well as food, and the word "grocery" was often used, sometimes mockingly, to indicate a store that the speaker considered a saloon in disguise.) Outside the grocery, Lucius Rountree, eager for some rough sport, urged another bystander, Jonathan Renno, to go into the place and "clean it out." Accepting the dare, Renno marched inside and took hold of the first man he saw, who was Randolph Britt. In the ensuing scuffle, Britt brandished a knife and began stabbing Renno, eventually plunging the knife into his throat. Renno reportedly cried out, "He is sticking me with a knife!" before he collapsed. According to George Escott's 1878 *History and Directory of Springfield and North Springfield*, Britt did not fully realize what had happened at first and deeply regretted his act once its full consequences sank in. R.I. Holcombe's 1883 county history added that, at the time of the incident, Britt was probably "so much intoxicated that he hardly knew what he was doing."

Britt was indicted for murder in April 1838 with both Rountree and McElhany among the witnesses for the prosecution. The following year, Britt was granted a change of venue to Benton County, where he was convicted of manslaughter. He returned to Greene County after serving a few years in the penitentiary at Jefferson City

An infamous lynching occurred in Springfield in the summer of 1859 after a black man was accused of raping a white woman. According to the *Springfield Mirror*, the wife of John Morrow was home alone on the night of August 20, when an unknown black man forced his way into her house by breaking down a door. The woman threw hot water on the intruder, but he overpowered and raped her. The woman immediately reported the incident to her neighbors, and a posse was soon formed. Several suspects were brought before Mrs. Morrow, but she failed to identify her attacker. A few days later, Martin (or Mart) Danforth, a slave who belonged to the estate of Josiah Danforth, became the primary suspect. On August 24, several days after the incident, the posse went to where Mart was working and managed to elicit a confession from him. (Mart was not working at the Danforth property, but he still belonged to the Danforth estate.)

According to the *Mirror*, "No force or threats were used to induce him to tell," but Mrs. Morrow identified him as her ravisher. Danforth was kept under guard and brought to Springfield the next day, where circuit court was in session at the time. The sheriff took charge of the prisoner, putting him under guard at the Temperance Hall on the east side of the square, and his case was going to be taken up that very day. However, a mob of about three or four hundred men gathered around the Temperance Hall, pushed their way in and took the prisoner out to the edge of town just east of where the Benton Avenue viaduct crosses Jordan Creek today. They put a rope around his neck and hanged him from a tree on the north side of the creek.

Only one case of prostitution was listed in the Greene County Circuit Court records prior to the Civil War. At the November 1852 term, Elizabeth Reed (also spelled "Read") was charged with keeping a bawdyhouse. Although a precise location was not given, one can assume the bordello was somewhere in Springfield, since there were no other sizeable towns in the county at this time. The charge specified that Ms. Reed did "on the first day of January and at divers other days" up to the finding of the indictment "keep a common bawdy house and did then and there permit divers men and women to the jurors unknown to commit whoredom. She, the said Elizabeth Read, then and there being the mistress of said house." Reed pled guilty to the charge in July 1853 and was fined $500, which was a princely sum in 1853. By comparison, defendants who were convicted of vices like gambling and illegal liquor sales (almost always men) were usually fined no more than $10. This disparity highlights an obvious Victorian double standard, by which women were expected to behave like ladies while men's peccadilloes were dismissed as boys being boys.

In contrast to prostitution, gambling was prevalent in Springfield almost from the town's beginning. In 1835, for instance, William Lloyd was indicted for keeping a faro bank. This is the only reference to faro in early Greene County Circuit Court records. However, there are numerous references to gambling devices or gambling tables, and it is safe to say that many of these pertain to faro, a card game that was very popular in gambling circles throughout the 1800s. The game usually involved a table with the thirteen cards of a single suit (normally spades) already painted or pasted on the tabletop. Players would place bets on one of the cards, and the dealer, using a separate deck of cards, would deal two cards from a device called a faro box, turning them face up one at a time. If the first card, called the dealer's or banker's card, matched the card on which the bet was placed, the player lost and the dealer collected the money. If the second card, called the player's card, matched the card on which the bet was placed, the player won and collected from the dealer or banker an amount equal to the bet. If neither card matched the card the bet was placed on, the player could retract his bet or let it ride for the next two-card turn. The term "faro bank" could refer to the stakes in a game of faro, to the gambling establishment where the game was played or to the game itself. The details of the charge against Lloyd, however, aren't known, as the defendant could not be found in Greene County. The charge was subsequently dropped.

Some of Springfield's leading citizens were involved in gambling. For example, John P. Campbell was charged in circuit court in 1841 with "suffering a gambling device to be set upon his premises." That same year, Benjamin Cannefax, brother of the second sheriff of Greene County, was found guilty of gaming and fined one dollar. Some of the other gambling offenders in early-day Greene County included John W. Ball, James Harper, John R. McFadden, Samuel B. Orr, Rodham K. Payne, Samuel Snow, Jeremiah B. Yancey and Ephraim and Levi Fulbright, sons of William Fulbright, who was one of the very earliest settlers in the area. Not surprisingly, some of these men were multiple offenders.

Gambling of any kind was at least nominally illegal in early-day Springfield, but in antebellum Greene County, the offense was made more serious if one gambled with the wrong person. For instance, at the December 1850 term of the Greene County Circuit Court, several men, including Fleming Taggard, were indicted for "gaming with a Negro." The following June, Taggard was again charged, this time with "playing cards with a Negro." Augustine Yokum was charged in December 1850 with the doubly grievous offense of "playing cards with a Negro on Sunday."

Early Springfieldians did not need a device specifically designed for games of chance in order to enjoy gambling. Holcombe's *History of Greene County* (1883) noted that many placed bets on the outcome of the 1855 elections. Betting on horse races was also a popular pastime in the mid- to late 1800s.

Like gambling, liquor violations were also common in early-day Springfield. In 1835, the year Springfield was founded, John Edwards was indicted for "retailing ardent spirits without a license." He was found guilty and fined twenty dollars. Other men brought before the court for liquor violations during the very early days of Springfield include William Dye and John Kirk.

As was true with gambling, dealing in liquor took on graver legal implications if nonwhites were involved. In the case of selling liquor, an otherwise legal activity automatically became a crime if the buyer wasn't white. For instance, both Joshua Jones and R.J. McElhany, who owned the grocery where Britt killed Renno, were indicted in Greene County in 1839 for selling liquor to Indians. In May 1850, Allen Fielden, who also ran a store on the public square, was charged with selling liquor to a slave. In the mid-1800s, exposing Indians or blacks to the demon whiskey was viewed much in the same way we view contributing to the delinquency of a minor today.

The vast majority of indictments involving liquor violations, according to Greene County Circuit Court records, were for either selling liquor without a license or selling liquor on Sunday. However, recurrent temperance crusades resulted in brief stretches during which liquor sales were banned altogether in Springfield, and merely "selling liquor" became a crime. One such crusade began in 1849 when a chapter of the Sons of Temperance, a brotherhood started in the United States during the 1840s that promoted temperance and utilized secret signs, passwords and hand grips, was organized in Springfield. After a two-year campaign by the Sons of Temperance and other Springfield prohibitionists, a petition was presented to the county court requesting that dram shops (i.e. saloons) be outlawed in the town, and a law to that effect was passed in October 1851. According to Holcombe's history, prior to the temperance movement taking hold in Springfield, "There had been a great deal of drunkenness and disorderly conduct in the place attributable, for the most part, to the dram shops and those who frequented them, and the people, aided especially by the Sons of Temperance, set about abating those institutions in order that peace and quietude might prevail and a potent evil removed from their midst."

The new law, however, did not stop the flow of whiskey in Springfield. In December 1851, for instance, just two months after the anti-dram shop ordinance became law, Jacob Baughman was indicted in circuit court on several counts of selling liquor, and there were apparently many Springfield residents besides Baughman who did not think liquor was a "potent evil." Aroused by the closing of the dram shops, the anti-prohibitionists soon presented a petition to the county court asking that the new law be rescinded, and the court took such an action on January 5, 1852. Five days later, however, when Allen Fielden applied for a dram shop license, the prohibitionists presented a petition to the court against the granting of the license, and the court denied the application, effectively withdrawing the law's repeal. The anti-prohibitionists now grew even more perturbed and began strongly agitating against the closure of the dram shops. Finally, in April 1852, the county court agreed to grant dram shop licenses at a cost of seventy-five dollars a year.

But the question of prohibition remained a contentious issue in Springfield throughout the prewar years. During 1856, the temperance advocates of Springfield, many of whom were women, continued to campaign for prohibition. They organized a petition drive and managed to bring the issue before the Missouri Legislature, and late in the year, the lawmakers passed what became known as the "Springfield liquor law," which forbade dram shops inside the city. In mid-December, the "ladies of Springfield" wrote to the legislators thanking them for enacting the law and reporting on the effects of its passage on Springfield: "There is now no dram-shop or grocery in Springfield—no licensed tempter of inconsiderate youth by the delusive elements of alcoholic beverages. And this city wears an aspect far different from what it did when dram shops were tolerated."

The Springfield liquor law spurred the anti-prohibitionists into action, and they presented a petition to their local state representative, William McFarland, asking that the law be rescinded. McFarland, believing most people were breaking the law and acquiring liquor illegally, presented a bill for repeal to the legislature in early 1857. The women of Springfield, however, forwarded a remonstrance to Jefferson City, and the bill did not pass, ensuring that the sale of liquor would remain illegal in Springfield, at least in theory, throughout the rest of the decade.

Prohibitionist editor J.W. Boren of the *Springfield Mirror* opined that McFarland was mistaken in believing that liquor was being obtained illegally in the city after passage of the Springfield liquor law, but the evidence documented in circuit court records suggests that McFarland might have been closer to the truth than Boren thought. At least eighty-six indictments for the illegal sale of liquor were handed down by the Greene County Circuit Court in March 1858 alone.

Illegal liquor sales continued in 1859. Holcombe's history noted that Greene County experienced financial difficulties during the latter part of the year, partly because of the extraordinary expenses it had encountered in prosecuting the numerous violators of the liquor law. As had been the case twenty years earlier, some of the liquor offenders in the late 1850s were prominent citizens of Springfield. For instance, John A. Stephens, who ran a dry-goods store on the square and had previously been a schoolmaster for about ten years, was one of many charged with selling liquor without a license at the March 1858 term of court. (Stephens was

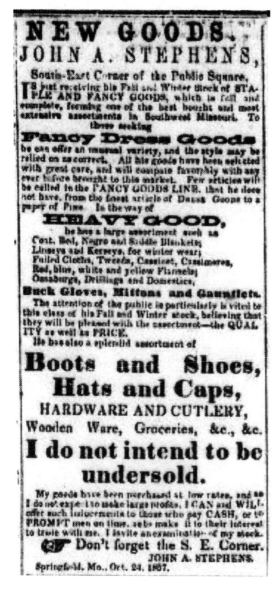

John A. Stephens's store on the public square sold more than "fancy dress goods" during the late 1850s. *Advertisement from the* Springfield Mirror, *1857.*

Courthouse on the public square at the northwest corner of College Street, built 1858. *From Fairbanks and Tuck's Past and Present of Greene County, Missouri.*

accidentally killed by Union soldiers during the Civil War, and his widow later became Springfield's first postmistress.)

Perhaps as widespread in early Springfield as gambling and liquor violations was what might be called general hell-raising. The raucousness, especially if it was fed by liquor, occasionally led to deadly consequences, like Britt's killing of Renno. However, most of the rowdiness resulted in nothing more serious than a misdemeanor charge against the offender.

By 1846, unruly conduct became a concern for Springfield city leaders, and the board of trustees passed a series of ordinances aimed at suppressing disruptive behavior. One such ordinance prohibited the firing of guns inside the city, while another prevented persons from running horses in the town. The trustees also saw blacks as a special threat to the peace and quiet of the town. An ordinance passed at the same time as the previous two banned the congregation of slaves inside the city "for the purpose of dancing, or for any other purpose except for public worship."

Despite the laws against disorderly conduct, there were still many instances of rowdy behavior and breaches of the peace. "Disturbing the peace of a family" and "disturbing the peace of a family at night" were common offenses brought before the circuit court throughout the 1850s. Nocturnal disturbances, in particular, became such a nuisance that the town council passed an ordinance in 1858 instructing the city marshal to arrest any person found loitering on the streets "at unusual hours." "Disturbing a neighborhood" and merely "disturbing the peace" were even more common offenses in 1850s Springfield than "disturbing the peace of a family." "Disturbing a religious assembly," "disturbing a public worship" and similar offenses that disrupted divine services were also frequent.

In 1860, the people of Springfield, along with the rest of the nation, turned their attention to the political battle being waged across two regions. Despite its history as a rough frontier town that had seen its share of violence and lawbreaking during its first twenty-five years, Springfield was still fairly calm by modern standards. Liquor was (technically) illegal, and crimes of moral turpitude were rare. Little did the townspeople realize that the looming war would not only tear the country apart but also forever change their rustic town.

Chapter Two

The Turbulent Civil War Era

D uring the first year of the Civil War, Springfield was essentially a combat zone, as the North and South vied to see which side would occupy the principal town of southwest Missouri. Vice and other crimes no doubt occurred during this time, but few records of such events survive, since the Greene County courts were not operating and few military records from the era remain. After the Union drove the Confederates out of Springfield in February 1862, life in the town, although still not normal, became less chaotic. Civil law was soon reestablished, and Federal martial law operated alongside the civilian courts. Surviving records, therefore, provide a clearer picture of life in Springfield during the latter part of the war than during the first year.

Perhaps the most notorious incident of the Civil War in Springfield that did not directly involve military operations occurred in the spring of 1862. Union sympathizer Mrs. Mary Willis, having lost two sons at the hands of bushwhackers in her home territory of northern Arkansas, sought refuge in Springfield, and she and her family were placed in a vacant house in the east part of town. Because the house had previously been occupied by what one observer called "a squad of accommodating girls," two soldiers were placed as guards at the house to turn away unwelcomed visitors. On May 21, duty officer John R. Clark and his orderly, A.J. Rice, drunkenly called at the Willis home and demanded dinner. When Mrs. Willis declined to prepare the meal, Clark and his companion became irate, pulled their pistols and tried to force their way into the house. One of the

Springfield public square looking southwest. *Sketch by Alexander Simplot, featured in* Harper's Weekly Magazine.

guards shot Clark through the body, and Clark staggered back a few steps and fell dead. Rice promptly fired at the guard but missed and hit Mrs. Willis's daughter, Miss Mary Willis, in the head, killing her instantly. The second guard then shot Rice, severely wounding him.

A Mexican War veteran, Clark was a member of the Fifth Kansas Cavalry, but he and his company had been recruited into Federal service from Mercer County, Missouri, where he had served four years as sheriff of the county and had been a delegate to the 1856 Democratic State Convention. Despite the circumstances of his death and despite the fact that he was considered by at least one member of his own regiment "a pro-slavery brute" who "ought to have joined the rebels instead of our side," Clark was buried in Springfield the day after his death and received both military and Masonic honors.

Upon initial examination, A.J. Rice's wound was considered fatal, but he lived long enough to be indicted the following summer for the murder of Miss Mary Willis. At the August 1862 term of court, he took a change of venue to Phelps County. He was tried there in late October and convicted on October 30 of first-degree murder. The next day, he filed an appeal, and he was granted a new trial on November 1. The case was continued the following April, but no record detailing its outcome has been found. According to Holcombe's 1883 *History of Greene County*, Rice's wound "eventually proved fatal," so it's possible he died before the new trial began.

Benjamin G. Andrews, whose family figured prominently in Springfield vice during the Civil War era, actually made his appearance in town a number of years before the war. He first shows up in circuit court records as a juror in a civil case in 1845. In 1853, Andrews, who ran a saloon at the southeast corner of the square, was granted a license to sell liquor, and the following year, he was indicted for the double offense of "selling whiskey to a slave on Sunday." In 1855, he was fined ten dollars for "gaming," and in 1856, he was charged several times with selling liquor without a license and once for "Sabbath breaking." In 1858 and 1859, during the height of the prewar temperance movement in Springfield, he was cited multiple times for selling liquor without a license.

By the time the war rolled around, Benjamin Andrews was over sixty years old, and his "career" in vice was winding down, but his sons took up where he left off. Eighteen-year-old Samuel Andrews was cited for gaming in 1853 and again the following year. In late 1860 or early 1861, he was involved in a fight and was later indicted for "felonious wounding." The charge was dropped in 1863, but he was indicted again (or the charge was possibly renewed) for felonious assault in 1864. He also faced multiple counts of gaming in 1864 and at least one count the following year.

The real rabble-rouser in the Andrews family, however, was Samuel's younger brother, Thomas. Near the beginning of the Civil War, when he was about nineteen or twenty years old, young Andrews took off for Colorado Territory. On his way back home in 1862, he was captured by Federal soldiers in St. Clair County, Missouri, and incarcerated at the Alton, Illinois military prison on suspicion of being a bushwhacker. Later that year, a number of Springfield citizens signed a petition testifying to Andrews's character and forwarded it to Federal authorities with a request that the young man be returned to Springfield to stand trial. Andrews himself swore that he had never been involved in the war, and his father made an oath supporting his son's assertion. The request to return Andrews to Springfield for trial was granted, and in 1863, he was acquitted of the charge.

It didn't take him long, however, to get in trouble again. One night in late December 1863, Andrews called at a home on South Jefferson Street where several women who had arrived in Springfield as refugees, including Agnes Crawford and her daughter Mollie, were living. When Mrs. Crawford answered the door, Andrews asked to see Mollie, but Mrs. Crawford turned him away. He came back the next night, however, drunk and in the company of several companions. They gathered outside the house and called for Mollie. Without waiting to be invited in,

Andrews kicked open the door, burst into the house and started toward Mollie's room. Mrs. Crawford jumped out of her bed and lit a lantern while Mollie shouted that she wanted something to kill Andrews with. She seized a fireplace poker while her mother grabbed a shovel, and together they forced the intruder back outside. However, he again kicked open the door, swearing, according to Mrs. Crawford, that he was going to "cut our God damned hearts out." The two women drove him back outside again, but he shoved his way through the door a third time, still swearing that he was going to cut out their hearts. He snatched the poker from Mollie and hit her with it before his companions interceded and led him away.

A few days later, Andrews came back to the Crawford house asking what he could do to make up for his boorish behavior. Mrs. Crawford told him all she wanted was for him to leave her and her daughter alone, but he kept coming back throughout the first three weeks of January, using "very insulting language" and otherwise bothering the Crawfords and the other women of the house until he was finally reported to the provost marshal of the Springfield post. He was arrested by military authorities on January 22, 1864, for disturbing the peace, but whatever punishment he received, if any, must have been mild. He was also charged in civil court with felonious assault, but the case was continued until the next term and eventually dropped.

Two months later, Andrews again bumped heads with the provost marshal, this time for illegally selling liquor. During 1862 and most of 1863, both civil and military authorities apparently took a somewhat more tolerant view toward alcohol sales in Springfield than the civil courts had during the prewar years. In November 1863, however, because of excessive drunkenness and the problems it brought with it, General John B. Sanborn, commander of the Southwest District, issued General Order No. 5, which made it illegal to sell intoxicating spirits to enlisted soldiers without a government permit. In late March 1864, Thomas Andrews, who now ran the family saloon at the southeast corner of the square, was charged with violating the order. Special military policemen Larkin Russell and James B. "Wild Bill" Hickok were among the witnesses who testified that they had seen soldiers drinking whiskey and brandy at the saloon.

As in the disorderly conduct case, Andrews was apparently let off with little punishment, because he was allowed to remain in the saloon business. On July 1, 1864, he paid a five-dollar tax to the provost marshal's office, which was a provision of General Order No. 9, a new military directive regulating the sale of liquor in Springfield and the surrounding area.

Although Andrews's tussles with the provost marshal were apparently over, his difficulties with civil authorities were not quite finished. He had already paid the Greene County Circuit Court a ten-dollar fine for gaming back in January 1864, which was around the same time he caused the disturbance at the house where the Crawfords were staying. At the July term of court, only days after he paid the liquor tax assessed by the military, he faced a whole slew of new indictments, including at least one count each of selling liquor without a license and selling liquor on Sunday and multiple counts of keeping a gambling device. On the charge of selling liquor on Sunday, Andrews was found not guilty. He was found guilty of selling liquor without a license, but he filed a motion for a new trial. He was also found guilty of keeping a gambling device and was ordered to pay a twenty-dollar fine and spend five minutes in jail as punishment.

James Harlow Fagg was another one of Springfield's prominent transgressors. Like Benjamin Andrews, Fagg made his appearance in Greene County records several years prior to the war, when he married Sarah Roberts in 1849. When Fagg first applied for a license to sell liquor in 1858, he was turned down, but this apparently did not deter him from pursuing the profitable business of peddling whiskey, as he was one of the many men indicted in circuit court in 1859 for selling liquor without a license. He paid a twenty-dollar fine for the violation.

James H. Fagg's primary occupation was tobacco manufacturer and seller, and during the war, he and partner Dewitt C. Brewster operated a store on St. Louis Street that doubled as a bowling saloon (also known as a ten-pin alley). Like Fagg, Brewster was brought before the court multiple times during the Civil War era for liquor violations and other minor offenses. Although Fagg's indictment for selling liquor without a license in 1859 was the last time he was cited for that particular offense in the county (at least until after the war), military records confirm that he continued to deal in liquor throughout the war.

After General Order No. 5 was issued in the fall of 1863, Brewster and Fagg continued to supply whiskey to soldiers without obtaining the necessary permit. They were also suspected of receiving some flour that had been stolen from the army. Near the end of the year, they were arrested, and their entire stock of goods was confiscated under the terms of the recent order. They appealed their case, but the testimony of soldiers and officers was against them. John Herrington, a soldier of the Sixth Cavalry Missouri State Militia, said he had purchased "spirituous liquors" at Fagg's ten-pin alley after Order No. 5 had gone into effect. Other testimony revealed that Brewster and Fagg had sometimes sold liquor to soldiers as late as three o'clock in the morning. In upholding the ruling against Brewster and Fagg, the provost marshal's office concluded, "The place which these men kept has long been a nuisance to the town, and soldiers could be seen at all times around there, and almost invariably intoxicated."

While the regulated sale of alcohol was allowed in Springfield during the Civil War, gambling of any kind was not. Although James H. Fagg was not cited in the county circuit court for selling liquor illegally during the war, he was indicted several times for gaming or keeping a gambling device and once for failing to appear as a witness in a gambling case against another man. As was often the case elsewhere, drinking and gambling tended to go hand in hand at Fagg's ten-pin alley.

The provost marshal had ordered Brewster and Fagg to cease operations and confiscated their stock, but this wasn't enough to stop Fagg. In May 1865, when the war was scarcely over, a soldier swore to military authorities that he had seen Fagg serve whiskey to another soldier. Then in 1867, Fagg was cited in circuit court for "selling liquor without an oath or bond" and again the following year for selling liquor without a license.

James H. Fagg died sometime before the 1870 census. His sons, however, quickly took up where their father left off, and they extended the family notoriety well beyond the Civil War. The oldest son, Joel Pinkney "Pink" Fagg, was indicted in Greene County in 1873 for playing cards on Sunday. In 1876, both he and his brother James V. "Bud" Fagg were charged with gambling.

Pink Fagg's first serious run-in with the law came in 1876, after he tried to rob gunsmith Jacob Painter by throwing a canister of chloroform into a room next to his shop on Olive Street while Painter was sleeping. The ruse backfired, however, and Fagg was arrested and indicted for attempted robbery. He was granted a change of venue to Christian County, where he was convicted and sent to the state penitentiary at Jefferson City. When he got out a couple of years later, he joined his brother Bud at Joplin, where both became notorious gamblers. In 1881,

Pink tried to kill his wife at Carthage, but the case was never brought to trial. He later served two more prison stints, one for felonious assault after shooting and wounding a man at a Fourth of July celebration in Pierce City and the other for manslaughter after killing a man on the streets of Fort Smith, Arkansas.

Pink and Bud's younger brother Alonzo Fagg was fatally stabbed by Samuel Means in Springfield while walking down South Street late on the night of April 19, 1879, after an evening of drinking at a nearby saloon. The two youngest Fagg brothers, Jack and Pete, also remained in Springfield, and each faced multiple gambling charges in the Greene County courts during the 1880s and 1890s.

Joseph F. O'Neal was another Springfield merchant who, like James H. Fagg, supplemented his income by dabbling in illegal pursuits. Although listed on the 1860 census as a shoemaker, O'Neal was charged with countless minor offenses involving alcohol during the Civil War years. Other frequent offenders of the city's liquor and gambling laws were Daniel Chandler, James Hays and John A. Page.

Druggists dispensed liquor for medicinal purposes during the 1800s, but they also often sold it without a prescription. For example, Ludwig Ullman, a "professed druggist" who ran a store on the east side of the Springfield public square during the latter part of the war, repeatedly got into trouble with both military and civil authorities for selling whiskey indiscriminately.

Some of Springfield's most prominent citizens were among the worst violators of the liquor laws during the Civil War just as they were before the war. William H. Worrell, for example, ran a "grocery" and confectionery on the west side of the square, while his wife, Sophia, ran a store on the south side of the square that was strictly a confectionery. Worrell was considered an upstanding member of the community, and his wife was one of the city's leading ladies. Worrell's business on the west side, however, doubled as a saloon, and he was cited repeatedly in circuit court from 1862 to 1865 for liquor violations. At the January 1864 term alone, he faced twelve separate indictments for "selling liquor without a license," and one soldier who testified in the case against Fagg and Brewster said that Worrell's store was another place where soldiers often obtained liquor illegally.

When the military clamped down on alcohol in Springfield in the fall of 1863, the civil authorities followed suit, and arrests for liquor violations

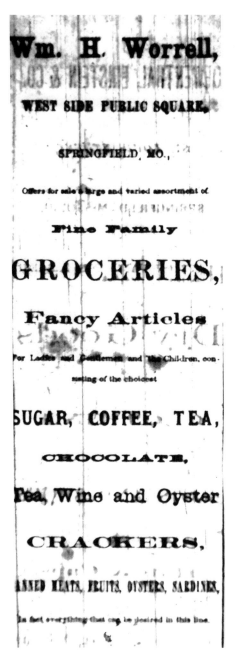

Wm. H. Worrell,

WEST SIDE PUBLIC SQUARE,

SPRINGFIELD, MO.,

Offers for sale a large and varied assortment of

Fine Family

GROCERIES,

Fancy Articles

For Ladies and Gentlemen and the Children, consisting of the choicest

SUGAR, COFFEE, TEA,

CHOCOLATE,

Tea, Wine and Oyster

CRACKERS,

CANNED MEATS, FRUITS, OYSTERS, SARDINES,

In fact, everything that can be desired in this line.

Worrell's establishment on the west side of the square reportedly sold more than groceries: it was also a saloon. *Advertisement from* the Springfield Missouri Weekly Patriot, *1865.*

spiked during the last two years of the war. Indeed, indictments became so numerous toward the end of the war that the circuit clerk at one point started his own system of shorthand by which frequent offenders were identified only by their initials. For instance, "WHW" (presumably William H. Worrell) was cited several times for "selling liquor without a license."

Although prostitution was virtually nonexistent in Springfield prior to the Civil War, the town became decidedly more scarlet during the war. Hundreds of refugees from southwest Missouri and northwest Arkansas flocked to the town, many of them women who had been abandoned or otherwise left on their own, and their abject poverty sometimes drove them to desperation. As Holcombe notes, "Vice and immorality of all sorts prevailed."

In October 1862, a Springfield man named J.P. Perkins complained to the provost marshal that a female refugee from Granby to whom he had rented a house had let some girls stay at the house. The girls reportedly "behaved in a manner unbecoming ladies," and he sought their eviction.

In May 1864, two men living near the college prison, located close to the intersection of Campbell and State Streets, complained of two

Springfield public square, circa 1865. Sophia Worrell's confectionery is on the right. *Courtesy Springfield–Greene County Library.*

"disorderly women," known only as Mrs. Rogers and Mrs. Whitstine, who had disrupted the neighborhood. The men claimed that Mrs. Whitstine had "abused respectable women…by shameful and indecent talk," that frequent quarrels among soldiers occurred near her house and that she and Mrs. Rogers were "public prostitutes." A former U.S. detective who was called to testify in the case confirmed that soldiers frequently visited the place for the purpose of having sexual intercourse and that Mrs. Rogers was a "base prostitute." The two women were declared public nuisances and banished from the District of Southwest Missouri.

On November 10, 1864, a woman named Mrs. Farmer was charged by the provost marshal with keeping a house of ill fame in Springfield and, like Mrs. Rogers and Mrs. Whitstine, was ordered out of the district. Mrs. Farmer's case was apparently not an isolated one. On November 12, two days after she was forced to leave town, another report was filed, noting, "Venereal disease prevails largely at this post and seriously effects [*sic*] the efficiency of our troops."

In December 1864, a Springfield man named Fielder complained of "a lewd family of women" who lived near his home. He said men in Federal uniforms regularly frequented the women's house and sometimes came to his place demanding food.

The provost marshal continued to receive complaints about lewd women in the Springfield area. In April 1865, a Mrs. Watkins gave a statement charging five women who lived near her with being public prostitutes and "encouraging soldiers into evil ways." In May, a man who lived two and a half miles north of Springfield near where some Federal soldiers were camped reported that several women who had taken up residence in a nearby cave "frequently become intoxicated and by their bad conduct attract the attention of the soldiers, who visit them very frequently."

Because of Springfield's status as a refugee camp, dubious men, as well as fallen women, flocked to the town. According to the *Springfield Journal,* by January 1865, the town was so overrun with scoundrels and petty criminals that most permanent citizens were afraid to leave their homes after dark for fear of being shot at or otherwise accosted.

When the Civil War ended, the people of Springfield, like the rest of the nation, marked the occasion in different ways. Some drank heavily and fired off guns in celebration, while others simply drew huge sighs of relief. Four long years of agonizing civil war were finally at an end. If any of them thought, however, that Springfield would ever go back to being the relatively innocent frontier town it had been before the war, they were mistaken.

Chapter Three

Wild Bill Hickok Makes
a Name for Himself

On the afternoon of July 21, 1865 (not the evening of July 20 as most accounts say), James Butler Hickok, Davis K. Tutt, James Orr and perhaps one or two other men were playing cards in Hickok's upstairs room at the Lyon House, a hotel located on the east side of South Street about two blocks off the square. As the game was breaking up, Tutt reminded Hickok of a prior debt, claiming that Bill, as the long-haired Hickok was often called, owed him thirty-five dollars. Hickok said the amount was only twenty-five dollars, telling Tutt that he had already paid ten dollars and had the correct amount written down in a memorandum. As he looked through his pockets for the note, Hickok pulled out his gold watch and laid it on the table. Tutt, who had just been bonded from jail the day before by a mutual acquaintance of his and Hickok's (and who was, no doubt, in desperate need of money), picked up the watch and announced that he would keep it until Hickok paid the thirty-five dollars. Hickok said that if Tutt would come downstairs with him, he would locate the memorandum and settle the debt, and the men got up to leave. Downstairs, Tutt said that the amount of the debt was actually forty-five dollars but he would take thirty-five. Hickok, though, insisted that he owed only twenty-five.

Hickok still could not locate his notation of the debt, and he, Tutt and Orr sat down on the porch outside the Lyon House to discuss the matter further. Eli Armstrong happened by and, learning of the quarrel, tried to act as a mediator. Hickok told Tutt he would rather have a dispute

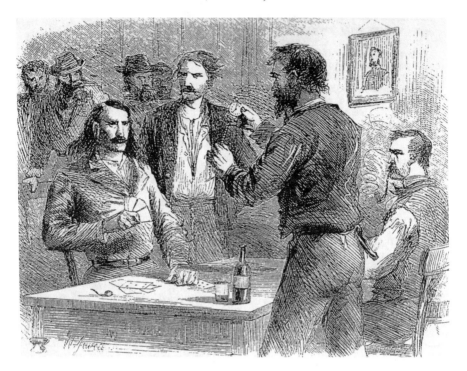

Depiction of the Hickok-Tutt poker game. *From* Harper's New Monthly Magazine.

with any man on earth than him because Tutt had accommodated him more than anybody else in town by lending him money when he needed it, and he reminded his friend that they had never had a fuss about the settlement before. Tutt said he felt the same way as Hickok and didn't want an argument either. Hickok offered to pay twenty-five dollars and the other ten if and when his memorandum book showed he owed it, and Tutt agreed to take thirty-five dollars instead of forty-five. Thinking the argument had been resolved, Armstrong announced, "Boys, that settles it." Hickok then suggested they all go inside the hotel and get a drink, and he and the other three men went into the Lyon House. Tutt gulped down a drink but left without returning Hickok's watch. Armstrong left shortly afterward, and Orr soon followed, leaving Hickok alone at the bar. It was about 5:00 p.m.

James Butler Hickok was only nineteen years old when he left his home in Homer (now Troy Grove), Illinois, in 1856 to make his way in the West, and he soon earned a reputation as a dashing, daring character. While working at an overland freight company, he was involved in a shootout

"Wild Bill" Hickok. *Courtesy Springfield–Greene County Library.*

that left three men dead at Rock Creek station in southeast Nebraska in the summer of 1861. In the fall of '61, Hickok signed on at Sedalia, Missouri, as a teamster for the Union army and later became a wagon master. He had started going by Bill before the war, and sometime during his tenure as a wagoner, he picked up the moniker Wild Bill. Later in the war, he landed in Springfield, where he was employed as a special policeman by the provost marshal of the post. Toward the end of the war, he became a scout and spy for General John B. Sanborn, commander of the Southwest District. Operating out of Springfield, Hickok roamed throughout southwest Missouri and into northwest Arkansas.

A native of Marion County, Arkansas, Davis K. Tutt was a descendant of the Tutt family known for their family feud with the Everetts, also of Marion County. In 1862, he joined the Confederate army but soon left the service. Around the end of 1863, he, his mother and the rest of the family came to Springfield as refugees from northern Arkansas.

Both Hickok and Tutt were known around Springfield as habitual gamblers and tough characters. Hickok was cited for playing a game called heads and tails, among other gambling charges, but he never appeared in court on any of the gaming charges, as he was always off on a scouting expedition and could not be found in Greene County. Sometime around January 1, 1864, the twenty-six-year-old Tutt was busted for gambling, but he put up a fight and ended up being charged with both gaming and resisting arrest. Another time, he was involved in a dispute over ownership of a horse.

Tutt and Hickok had known each other for several months, if not a couple of years, prior to their gambling quarrel, and they both kept company with the same group of men. In January 1865, for instance, Tutt had joined Hickok, John H. Jenkins and Thomas G. Martin, a former scouting partner of Hickok, in securing Larkin Russell's release on bond after Russell, who had been a policeman for the provost marshal at the same time as Hickok, was arrested for grand larceny. On July 20, 1865, the day before the dispute at the Lyon House, Tutt had been fined $100 for resisting arrest and was unable to pay. His friend Thomas Martin, however, arranged his release. Hickok and Tutt then were among a coterie of friends who gambled together and helped each other out when they got in trouble.

Despite what friendship the two may have had, their quarrel on that July afternoon changed everything. After leaving the Lyon House, Tutt walked downtown to the livery at the northwest corner of the square. Following the departure of Tutt and the other two men, Hickok also wandered toward the square and stationed himself at its intersection with South Street, waiting for Tutt to come back across the square. A couple of men happened by and asked Hickok what was going on. Hickok explained his dispute with Tutt and told them he had better not see Tutt come across the square wearing his watch and that if he did, there would be hell to pay. Hickok then cautioned the two men that they might want to move along and get out of harm's way.

About 6:00 p.m., Orr, who had gone home briefly, came back downtown and stopped at the corner to talk to Hickok. Hickok suggested that Orr find Tutt and tell him that Hickok was prepared to pay him the twenty-five dollars as soon as Tutt brought the watch back, adding that if he didn't return it, "something else would be done." Orr balked at carrying out the assignment, and Hickok accused him of taking Tutt's side in the argument. He warned Orr, as he had the previous two men, to clear away from there, but Orr said he had as much right to the street as anybody else.

Orr finally ambled on, but other men continued to walk by and stop to talk to Hickok, one of whom was Tutt's brother. Tutt's brother told Hickok he was sorry to hear about the difficulty between Bill and Dave and expressed confidence that the two men could make amends. But the time for negotiation had already passed.

Moments later, Hickok spotted Tutt starting across the square from the northwest corner, and he walked out a few steps to meet him. As Tutt drew closer to the courthouse, Hickok shouted for him not to come any farther while wearing Hickok's watch, but Tutt wouldn't back down. The two men halted about seventy-five yards apart and went for their pistols, drawing and firing at about the same time. Tutt missed, but Hickok didn't. The bullet pierced Tutt's side, and he staggered back toward the courthouse, collapsed in the doorway and died within a minute or two.

After the shooting, bystander Fred W. Scholten remarked to Bill that his actions had been "rather hard," but Hickok replied that it was too late now and he wasn't sorry for what he had done. He surrendered his

A depiction of the gunfight between Hickok and Tutt. *From* Harper's New Monthly Magazine.

Springfield square as it appears today. *Photo by author.*

weapon and turned himself in to military authorities. He was handed over to the county sheriff shortly afterward.

Meanwhile, Tutt's body was taken to his mother's house on South Street, where a coroner's inquest was begun almost immediately. Eyewitness testimony was collected the following day, and the jury concluded that "Davis K. Tutt came to his death by a pistol shot" and that "the said violence causing said death was committed by a certain James B. Hickock [*sic*]." Tutt was buried at the city cemetery at the corner of State and Campbell Streets, but his body was later disinterred and moved to Maple Park.

Hickok was indicted for manslaughter and tried at the Greene County Circuit Court in early August 1865 before Judge Sempronius H. "Pony" Boyd. Robert W. Fyan served as the prosecuting attorney, and John S. Phelps represented the defendant. Fyan asked the judge to instruct the jurors that, in order to find Hickok not guilty by reason of self-defense, they must believe that he not only did not provoke the encounter but also that he tried to avoid it. If he willingly engaged in the conflict, Fyan argued, or if it was in any way premeditated, the jury must find Hickok guilty. Fyan also asked that the judge instruct the jurors to not

Photograph of Davis Tutt's grave at Maple Park Cemetery in Springfield. *Photo by author.*

consider Tutt's moral character, his reputation for loyalty or any threats he might have made against Hickok prior to the Lyon House dispute. Judge Boyd, however, told the jury that if they believed Tutt advanced on the defendant with his pistol drawn, had previously made threats against Hickok and had a reputation as a fighting man, these circumstances constituted grounds for reasonable doubt and they must acquit Hickok.

The jury apparently gave more weight to the judge's instructions than to Fyan's argument. On Saturday, August 5, they returned a verdict of not guilty by reason of self-defense. According to the following week's *Missouri Weekly Patriot*, the public was dissatisfied with the verdict and was outraged that "a man could arm himself and take a position at a corner of the public square, in the centre of the city, and await the approach of his victim for an hour or two, and then willingly engage in a conflict with him which resulted in his instant death" and yet be found not guilty of manslaughter. Holcombe notes that when the verdict was first announced, a prominent attorney denounced it from the balcony of the courthouse as contrary to the evidence presented at the trial and to human decency and that some of the bystanders reportedly talked of lynching Hickok.

Seeking to shield Judge Boyd from the public outcry, the August 10 edition of the *Weekly Patriot* claimed that the judge had "conducted himself impartially throughout the trial." In a dubious attempt to prove the judge's objectivity, the newspaper cited the instructions that Fyan had requested Boyd to pass on to the jury and falsely identified them as the instructions Boyd actually delivered to the jury. The newspaper further stated that those who claimed to be so outraged by the alleged crime and who were so dissatisfied with the verdict were partly to blame for standing idly by while the events leading up to the gunfight unfolded.

Many of those upset by the Hickok verdict were former Confederates or Confederate sympathizers who felt the trial proceedings had been colored by the loyalty issue, and there was very likely some truth to their accusation. Because of the Drake Constitution that was passed in Missouri at the close of the Civil War, no one who had ever been a member of the Confederate army or a known Confederate sympathizer could serve on a jury without first taking an oath of allegiance, something that many unrepentant Rebels were unable to do. Therefore, all the jurors in the Hickok case were pro-Unionists, and all of them no doubt were aware that Hickok was a former Union scout while Tutt was an ex-Confederate. Additionally, all three of the trial officials (Boyd, Fyan and Phelps) were former Union officers, and the editors of the *Weekly Patriot* were strong pro-Unionists as well. While all those involved in the trial might have paid lip service to impartiality, it's fair to say, to use a gambling metaphor, that the deck was stacked in Hickok's favor.

Regardless of whether justice was blind in *State of Missouri v. James B. Hickok*, the only thing that ultimately mattered to Hickok was that he walked out of the courthouse a free man. A month later, he ran for Springfield city marshal and finished as the runner-up with 63 votes. The winner garnered 107 votes, while three other candidates received a combined total of 61. Although it would probably be a mistake to read too much into the results, the election totals show, especially when we keep in mind that unapologetic Rebels were not allowed to vote, that Wild Bill's shootout with Dave Tutt had not made him a hero in Springfield.

Near the time of the city election, Colonel George Ward Nichols arrived in Springfield to write a highly exaggerated version of the Tutt gunfight (along with stories of Wild Bill's other escapades) for *Harper's New Monthly Magazine*. According to Nichols's version of Hickok's exploits, Bill single-handedly killed ten men during the Rock Creek affair at the beginning of the Civil War. In truth, only three men died, and it's unclear whether or not Bill personally killed any of them. Dubbed "Captain Honesty" in the *Harper's* article, Captain R.B. Owen, who, as assistant quartermaster of the Southwest District, had occasionally employed Hickok during the war, introduced the writer from the East to the daring scout. Bill was apparently a willing partner in the author's embellished account of his deeds. As Hickok scholar Joseph G. Rosa has noted, Hickok himself planted some of the seeds that eventually grew into a myth of gigantic proportions.

In January 1866, Hickok was a witness to the killing of James Coleman by Springfield policeman John Orr on South Street near the Lyon House, and he was one of several men who gave testimony at the subsequent coroner's inquest into Coleman's death. Orr was accused of using undue force, but he skipped town after he was released on bail and was never recaptured.

Not long after the Coleman killing, Hickok, at the request of Captain Owen, left Springfield for Fort Riley, Kansas, where Owen had been appointed acting quartermaster. There, Hickok worked as a government detective. When Nichols's article finally appeared in late January 1867, Wild Bill Hickok became a legend, although back in Springfield, the editors of the *Weekly Patriot* scoffed at Bill's supposed derring-do and had scathing words for Nichols, whom the newspapermen remembered mainly for frequenting saloons and "endangering the supply of lager and core whiskey" during his brief stay fourteen months earlier. Most of the people of Springfield who read the *Harper's* article fell into "convulsions of laughter." There were a few, however, who were indignant that Nichols had portrayed their town as a backward, uncivilized place.

Hickok's adventures as a lawman and army scout over the next few years only enhanced his celebrity. However, when he returned to Springfield in the fall of 1872 for what is thought to be his only visit after 1866, his presence was scarcely noted, at least in the local press. Bill stayed at the St. James Hotel on South Street until August 1873, when he went east to join Buffalo Bill Cody's Wild West Show.

By the time Jack McCall shot Hickok in the back of the head in Deadwood, South Dakota Territory, on August 2, 1876, Wild Bill had become the most famous figure in the American West. Again, however, the Springfield newspapers paid little attention. The *Weekly Patriot* merely recounted a Chicago newspaper's account of the murder, while D.C.

Kennedy, editor of the *Springfield Leader* and a former Confederate soldier, considered Bill Hickok's passing unworthy of mention.

By the 1920s, however, as Hickok's fame continued to grow posthumously, many of Springfield's older citizens were more than eager to share their real and imagined recollections of Wild Bill's exploits in Springfield and southwest Missouri. Some of the storytellers weren't even born at the time of the infamous Tutt gunfight, and several painted very negative pictures of Hickok, perhaps venting some of the anti-Hickok sentiment that arose in the wake of the Tutt verdict and that still lingered sixty years later.

In 1975, small metal plaques were placed in the street in Park Central Square marking the approximate locations where Davis Tutt and Wild Bill Hickok stood when they drew down on each other in July 1865. The Tutt plaque is just north of where College Street enters the square, and the Hickok plaque is just east of where South Street enters the square, although Hickok's actual position was farther west and slightly south of the current marker.

Chapter Four

The Stirring Sixties and the Spirited Seventies

S pringfield bustled with activity in the years immediately after the Civil War. Telegraph service had reached the town just before the war started, and a railroad was in the works by the time it ended. By early 1866, people were flooding to southwest Missouri by stagecoach or wagon in search of cheap land. According to the *Weekly Patriot*, the town was "full of strangers," and the hotels and boardinghouses were overflowing. The newspaper's editor claimed that he could look outside his office at "almost any hour of the day" and find the streets full of people mingling downtown or passing through on their journey westward. But with the influx of people came an increase in crime and vice.

Despite periodic efforts to control the sale of liquor in Springfield, such as the anti–dram shop ordinance adopted in early 1866, whiskey flowed freely from the town's saloons, and alcohol continued to play a part, as it had before the war, in much of the raucous behavior and many of the rough scrapes that took place in the post–Civil War era. Some of the scrapes proved fatal, such as when Kindred Rose mortally wounded James Simpson with a blow to the head in a Springfield saloon in February 1867, or when Perry Lewis shot and killed Samuel Massey at a brothel on the northwest edge of town the following month. More often, excessive intake of spirits contributed to fistfights and stabbing affrays that left the combatants battered or severely wounded but alive. Most of the time, liquor led to nothing more serious than boisterous and unruly behavior that landed the participants in the calaboose for a night or two.

On Saturday, September 21, 1865, the *Weekly Patriot* reported that twelve men had been arrested the previous Monday for being drunk and disturbing the peace. Another five were arrested for public drunkenness and disturbing the peace the next day, what the paper called "a decided falling off from Monday, caused by the efficiency of our very worthy City Police." Three more arrests were made on Wednesday, and on August 29, 1867, the editor of the newspaper reported that, although he had often heard of women getting drunk, he had never witnessed one in that condition until the previous day, when he had seen two "as drunk as whiskey could make them" as they were being hauled off to jail.

On March 28, 1868, a fight broke out at the Humboldt Saloon, located on the west side of the square next to the courthouse. Patrick Daly, described by the *Weekly Patriot* as "a quiet, peaceable citizen," reportedly got drunk and assaulted the bartender, James M. Kirby, with a knife. The barkeeper picked up a beer glass and threw it at his attacker, striking him in one of his eyes and bursting his eyeball.

Another brawl took place at the Humboldt less than two years later, the results of which proved fatal. Michael Connery and Owen Monday got into a dispute at the saloon around Christmas of 1869, and the argument resumed when they met each other back at the Humboldt on the night of January 1, 1870. Connery promptly drew a knife and fatally stabbed Monday in the neck. Kirby witnessed the fight and provided Mayor William Gilmore with a statement two days later. William Cannefax's murder of Harrison Lindenbower in January 1871 also occurred at the Humboldt, but alcohol apparently played little, if any, part in the crime.

James Kirby was one of Springfield's most notorious saloonkeepers during the latter part of the nineteenth century. He moved his business to the south side of College Street in the early 1870s. In 1874, several citizens complained to the town council about "the obscene and profane conversation of men who hover in front of J.M. Kirby's saloon." In 1877, Kirby moved his establishment to South Street, and in the spring of 1879, Alonzo Fagg was killed just outside the saloon. He moved his saloon a few more times over the next several years to other locations in the downtown area, and the business, regardless of where it was located, continued to be a magnet for rough characters. Kirby was also cited for various gambling and liquor violations during the latter 1800s.

Of course, many citizens in 1860s Springfield opposed saloons altogether, and temperance continued to be a hotly contested issue, just as

An advertisement for James M. Kirby's saloon. *From the* Springfield Leader, *1874.*

it was before the war. In the mayoral campaign of 1868, rival newspapers the *Springfield Leader* and the *Weekly Patriot* debated whether or not either one of the candidates—William Gilmore or J.B. Dexter—frequented saloons or, worse yet, owned an interest in one. Another temperance crusade arose in late January 1869 when the Baptist Sabbath School decided, in the words of the *Leader,* "to arrest the tide of intemperance in our city," and the Temperance Society of Springfield was formed on February 1. Late the next night, Charles Lack's saloon was set on fire, but the blaze was extinguished in time to save the structure. It's possible Lack was targeted not only because he owned a saloon but also because he was suspected to have been involved in a scandalous incident. The previous June, he had been charged in circuit court as an accessory in a case of "abominable and detestable crimes against nature" brought against Anna Wagoner for encouraging the woman to have "carnal connections with a dog."

Throughout the late 1860s, the people of Springfield looked forward to the day when a railroad would link their town to the rest of the country. Progress toward the goal was slow, and at one point in 1867,

Commercial Street Depot about thirty years after its construction. *Courtesy Springfield–Greene County Library.*

a St. Louis newspaper suggested that those in charge of the project were just as likely to build a railroad to the moon as to Springfield. The long-awaited railroad finally came on April 22, 1870, when the track of the South Pacific Railroad reached the Springfield depot, located in a sparsely populated area about a mile north of the public square. The railway, however, was not as close to the business district as many Springfieldians would have liked. Additionally, a rival town named North Springfield (which some facetiously called Moon City and which later would commonly be referred to as North Town) soon established itself around the depot. The town mainly catered to railroad travelers and featured hotels, boardinghouses, saloons and a variety of other businesses, all of which were located, for the most part, along Commercial Street, the town's main thoroughfare. Moon City would soon compete with Springfield's businesses as well as become a hotspot for vice and crime.

After a man named Packett was knocked down and robbed near the depot on the night of June 2, 1870, the *Springfield Leader*, in reporting the incident, remarked that the "amount of lawlessness in the celestial premises" was increasing and that the denizens of Moon City wished to establish their own police force. According to the *Weekly Patriot*, another man was similarly accosted and robbed three nights later on north Boonville Street by "roughs from about the depot."

In 1871, another notorious lynching occurred in Springfield under circumstances very similar to the 1859 Danforth lynching. On June 19, Martha Christian, a twenty-year-old white woman, was reportedly attacked by a black man at her home in the south part of Springfield. Her assailant was immediately identified as Bud Isbell, and her husband, thirty-eight-year-old Peter Christian, offered a $100 reward for Isbell's arrest. Later that week, the fugitive was captured in Newton County and brought back to Springfield on Saturday, June 24. He was first taken to the Christian residence, where Martha identified him as the man who had outraged her, and then marched to the public square. A large crowd soon gathered, and after some consultation, the mob decided to take Isbell "into the Jordan valley" and hang him. He was herded out to a spot just east of Benton Avenue, right across the creek bank from where Mart Danforth had been lynched twelve years earlier. He was placed on a horse, and a rope that was tied to a tree limb was looped around his neck. The horse was led out from under him, but when he dropped, the rope was too long, so his feet ended up touching the ground, and he was only partially choked. The crowd lifted him up while someone adjusted the rope to make it shorter, and Isbell was soon "swinging between heaven and earth," according to the *Leader*. Before he died, however, someone pulled out a pistol and shot him in the head, finishing off what the rope had begun. A coroner's inquiry into the lynching named three men who had participated in the mob action, but no one was ever charged in the crime.

Prostitution increased in the years after the railroad line was established, not just in the "lunar" part of Springfield but throughout the whole town. In the spring of 1872, a member of the city council argued that regulating the number of bawdyhouses within the city was entirely necessary and needed to be done with the utmost swiftness. The council, however, adjourned without taking any action. In March 1874, the council finally passed an ordinance that instructed the city marshal or police officers to "enter any bawdy house or assignation house, or any house or room used for the purposes of prostitution, in the city…upon the information or complaint of any credible person and arrest without process all persons found therein." But effects of the ordinance were not immediate. A week after the ordinance was passed, the *Weekly Patriot* reported that certain parties had been fined one dollar for keeping a bawdyhouse in Jasper County and remarked, "They do it in Springfield without any fine." However, less than four months later, the same newspaper reported that George Downs had been fined five dollars for keeping a bawdyhouse in Springfield. Letha Gideon and Martha Kelley were also cited for keeping bawdyhouses in 1874.

Martha Wallace, who ran a brothel for many years with co-madam Belle Wilson near the corner of Commercial and Lyon Streets in North Springfield, was first indicted in 1875. She and Belle faced multiple charges of keeping a bawdyhouse throughout the late 1870s and into the early 1880s. The whorehouse was enumerated in the 1880 census, and forty-year-old Martha Wallace was listed as the head of household. Under "occupation" was written "house of bad repute." Thirty-nine-year-old Belle Wilson was listed as one of the "inmates." The other six

An 1877 warrant for the arrest of Belle Wilson, who was charged for keeping a bawdyhouse. *Courtesy Greene County Archives and Records Center.*

women in the house varied in age, from nineteen-year-old Lizzie Gray to thirty-year-old Mollie May. Martha Wallace vanished from Springfield's prostitution scene sometime in the early 1880s, but Belle Wilson carried on throughout the decade and into the next.

On June 6, 1875, a deadly knife fight occurred at a residence in the south part of Springfield, which Holcombe's history later identified as "Annie Boyer's house of ill fame." Annie was apparently entertaining several men at the same time when one of them, Amos Cooper, started an argument with a second one, R.C. Taylor, who was the superintendent of Springfield National Cemetery. Cooper, who, according to the *Weekly Patriot*, was "pretty full of whisky," slashed Taylor with a knife while holding off Annie and a third man with a pistol to keep them from intervening.

In late February 1876, indignant citizens vandalized a bawdyhouse in North Springfield. The March 2 edition of the *Weekly Patriot* reported, "The soiled doves who so long held high carnival there have flown—whither no one knows or cares." At the May term of the Greene County Circuit Court, a charge of keeping a bawdyhouse against Mollie Fisher was nol-prossed, perhaps because she was one of the birds that had flown. If so, her next stop, contrary to the *Patriot*'s assertion, is known; Molly landed in Joplin shortly after taking flight and became a notorious madam in the booming mining town during the late 1870s.

Although most of nineteenth-century Springfield's rough scrapes occurred in saloons or brothels, not all of them did. On Christmas night in 1876, twenty-year-old Charles Layton shot and killed eighteen-year-old Bion Mason at a house on St. Louis Street, where a number of young people had gathered to have a party (or what Holcombe called a "low dance"). The assailant, of course, was reportedly drunk at the time.

Indeed, one of the main reasons for the temperance crusades was that liquor contributed to so many murders, assaults and lesser crimes. However, it is fair to add that most people in the nineteenth century used alcohol as a facilitator of recreation and merrymaking without its leading to dire consequences, just as they do today. Most saloons in Springfield, as elsewhere, offered various forms of auxiliary entertainment in addition to the lure of intoxicating spirits. Some of the saloons, of course, served as fronts for illegal gambling operations, and almost all of them featured inducements such as billiard tables or bowling alleys. Around May 1, 1877, Henry Scholten installed a new billiard table at his saloon, which was located near the corner of Patton Avenue and present-day McDaniel

Street. According to the *Leader*, it was a "new and handsome 16 ball pool table, which will afford much sport to those who delight in billiard games."

Some saloonkeepers tried to oblige nondrinkers. When James Kirby moved from College Street to South Street in September 1877, his new saloon featured a bowling alley that was housed in an adjoining building so that those "with conscientious scruples against going into saloons" could enter it without having to walk into the saloon. Henry Scholten's brother Emanuel went so far as to quit serving alcoholic beverages, and he renamed his establishment the Temperance Saloon. "Needless to say, it is a novelty to see a temperance saloon in Springfield," read an article in the *Missouri Weekly Patriot*.

Perhaps even more so than today, beer during the 1800s was viewed in a different light than hard liquor, as indicated by this excerpt from an 1876 article published in the *Leader*: "Beer, if not a temperance drink, is certainly a temperate one—a fact admitted by total abstinence men." The main supplier of beer in Springfield during the 1870s was the

E. T. SCHOLTEN,

BILLIARD HALL

AND BOWLING ALLEY,

SOUTH ALLEY, NEAR THE SQUARE.

One of the most private saloons in the city, and will give parties for amusement in TEN-PINS, BILLIARDS, OR CARDS, the utmost attention.

The bar is supplied with the best of Liquors, not surpassed by any in the city. Remember A GRAND LUNCH every Saturday. Give me a call and I will give you satisfaction in every way.

Advertisement for Emanuel Scholten's billiard hall and ten-pin alley shortly before it became a temperance saloon. *From the 1873–1874 Springfield City Directory.*

Southwest Brewery, located on College Street near its intersection with Fort Street. Built in 1872 by Philip Finkenauer, the brewery turned out almost one thousand barrels a day and, at one point in 1876, had about sixteen thousand gallons stored in a cellar. Later that year, Sebastian Dingeldein acquired the brewery and helped increase its output. In 1877, however, someone tried to burn the brewery down. Beer might have been a temperate drink, as the *Leader* maintained, but it was not immune from the attacks of zealous temperance crusaders.

Despite their proximity to a productive brewery, some of the local saloons continued to import beer from other cities. Henry Scholten, for instance, advertised his establishment as Springfield's exclusive dealer in Cincinnati lager, which he sold for twenty cents a bottle or two dollars a dozen.

A new temperance campaign called the Murphy Movement hit the Springfield area in early 1878. Previous temperance crusades had, for the most part, targeted saloons with the aim of getting laws passed that prohibited or restricted the sale of alcohol, but the Murphy Movement targeted the drinkers themselves by persuading them to sign abstinence pledges and then giving them blue ribbons to wear as symbols of their vows. The movement held its first Springfield meeting on January 28 at the Christian Church, located at the corner of College and Campbell, and over 200 people signed the pledge the first night. The movement gained momentum over the next several days, and by February 6, approximately 1,900 people had taken the pledge in Springfield. On February 14, the *Springfield Leader* reported that only three or four drinks had been sold in one of the local saloons the previous Saturday, and the next week, the same newspaper remarked that the whiskey business "continues dull." Even the saloonkeepers admitted that the Murphy Movement had put a damper on their business. However, one saloonkeeper told the *Springfield Times* that the only customers he had lost were "those afraid to be seen coming from a saloon while the excitement is at its height," and he predicted that the saloon business would soon pick up again.

As previously indicated, there was somewhat of a gender divide in regard to the liquor issue during the late 1800s. The *Leader* reported on April 4, toward the end of the Murphy Movement, that Sophia Worrell had recently hosted a lunch for the Temperance Union at her confectionery store. Her former husband, who had died several years earlier, was one of the worst offenders of the liquor laws during the Civil War era, and indeed, the liquor issue might well explain why the couple had kept separate stores. Ironically, Sophia's temperance luncheon was held in early April, just around the time Springfield's saloon business started to revive.

Two months later, in June 1878, the editor of the *Springfield Patriot-Advertiser* lamented over the "cooling off of the ardor" of the Murphy Movement within the city. Indeed, by the following year, things were pretty much back to normal; men were once again getting drunk and killing each other in saloons, while visitors to bawdyhouses and brothels filled themselves and their dames with liquor and made merry. On Christmas Eve in 1879, a rough character named John Vaughan, while drinking in a North Springfield saloon, showed "a disposition to bully and intimidate" another customer and even flourished a revolver in a threatening manner. The saloonkeeper, H.C. Roberts, intervened and reprimanded Vaughan for his behavior, but then he immediately turned away to attend to another task. Vaughan promptly pointed the pistol toward Roberts and shot him in the back. The bullet lodged itself near the base of the spine, killing him almost instantly. Vaughan was arrested and went to trial the following year, but he was acquitted on grounds of insanity.

Chapter Five

The Outlaw Eighties

A round 10:30 p.m. on the night of August 6, 1880, eight black men walked into William Potter's saloon on Boonville Street and ordered beer. They were served, and after they had drunk the beer, they asked for a free lunch, which Potter usually provided to his regular customers. Potter refused, and the dispute that followed quickly turned into a mêlée, as shots were fired and beer glasses were thrown. One bullet struck Potter in the hip, but the wound was not considered life threatening. Out of the eight black men who were arrested, only five were charged for starting a fight, but soon afterward, they were released on bail.

The shooting scrape at Potter's saloon was just one of many such incidents that took place in Springfield saloons during the 1880s. Although alcohol-related violence was not uncommon in previous decades and had come to be more or less accepted as a byproduct of drinking in saloons, the number of drunken brawls seemed to spike upward during the decade of the eighties.

On the evening of September 16, 1882, Mike Ahern and Payton Parrish got into a fight at Nat Kinney's Boonville Street saloon, where they had been drinking most of the day. Ahern reportedly became aggressive and knocked Parrish down and then jumped astride the smaller man and continued to pummel him as he lay on the floor. Parrish was able to pull a knife from his pocket, and he plunged it into Ahern's stomach several times in quick succession. Ahern was taken to a nearby boardinghouse and died shortly thereafter. Parrish was arrested but released on bail,

Photograph of Springfield bartender Nat Kinney. *Courtesy Christian County Library.*

and no indictment was brought against him, as the killing was considered self-defense. When interviewed in November by a grand jury about the killing, Kinney claimed he "didn't know who done it."

On December 26, 1882, police officer James Dameron got into a row with a barber named Henry Herndon at Abel Kinney's Bank Saloon near the northwest corner of the public square. Dameron shot Herndon during the struggle, and the barber died a few days later. The officer was discharged on grounds of justifiable homicide.

Abel (A.F.) Kinney ran a saloon in Springfield as early as the late 1860s. His younger brothers, John Charles F. Kinney and Oliver R. Kinney, tended bar in the saloon, and John later opened his own. Although Nat Kinney worked at the Kinney saloon on the square for a brief time, the exact kinship between Nat and the other Kinneys is unknown. Not long after the 1882 fight between Parrish and Ahern, Nat moved to Taney County and became leader of the notorious Bald Knobbers. The three brothers, meanwhile, stayed in Springfield and were cited for multiple liquor violations, including "selling liquor without a license," "selling liquor to minors" and "keeping open a dram shop on Sunday."

Sometime around 1880, James M. Kirby moved his saloon from South Street to a walkway at the southwest corner of the public square, which connected the square to South Alley (which is now McDaniel Street). The passage came to be known as the Kirby Arcade. In early 1883, he opened a second saloon on the north side of College Street at the corner of Patton Alley. In mid-February, the *Springfield Patriot* reported that new fixtures to furnish the saloon were arriving daily. The editor noted wryly that Kirby's new business would be "gorgeous—a miniature palace, where the love of art and the love of beer can be gratified at a minimal cost. Art and beer mingle gracefully." Apparently, however, the palatial surroundings had no effect on Kirby's clientele. On the night of February 28, just a few weeks after the grand opening, John Conroy and Jack Griffin were drinking at the new saloon when they got into an argument, and Conroy allegedly called Griffin a "son of a bitch." Griffin, who, according to the *Springfield Express*, had long been "noted for his general cussedness and worthlessness to the community," immediately whipped out his pistol and shot Conroy, killing him. Griffin fled but was later captured, brought back for trial and given a fifty-year prison sentence.

On the night of October 4, 1883, beer dealer Jacob Walter got into a "friendly scuffle" with J.F. Atzert and Fred Winkle at Scott and Good's saloon at 221 Boonville and suffered what he apparently thought was nothing worse than a minor beating. Battered and bruised, Walter staggered home but died almost two weeks later from swelling of the brain and cerebral hemorrhaging caused by the blows to the head he had received. Atzert and Winkle were arraigned, but the grand jury failed to indict.

Winkle later became a saloonkeeper himself, operating Schoner and Winkle's saloon at 315 Boonville Street with partner Paul Schoner. He would also be indicted several times during the early 1890s for liquor violations, one of which was opening the saloon on a Sunday. He was also charged at least once for keeping a gambling house and was separately charged for keeping a bawdyhouse.

Another fatal altercation occurred at A.F. Kinney's saloon on June 23, 1884. Prior to the fight, William Chapman had allegedly sexually assaulted T.C. Asbridge's sister-in-law. Asbridge confronted Chapman and, during the encounter, cut him several times with a knife. Chapman was carried home in a wagon and died a day or two later. Asbridge was released on the grounds of self-defense.

Not all barroom disturbances that took place during this decade proved fatal. An article in a July 1883 issue of the *Weekly Patriot* described how four "ambitious kids just entering upon the threshold of manhood and just now awakening to the ineffable pleasure and incomparable honor to be gained by dissipation and debauchery" created a panic at John Isley's beer garden in North Springfield when they started throwing chairs at another customer, causing all the other customers to run for cover, knocking over tables and lamps in their wild flight.

Saloonkeeper James M. Kirby was involved in several other confrontations over the course of the decade. In November 1882, he reportedly knocked down one of his customers in a dispute over a nickel. Sometime around July 1, 1889, he and Conrad Price, who was supposedly a good friend of Kirby's, got into a fight while they were drinking together at a billiard hall. According to testimony, Kirby knocked Price down, hit him again while he was down and, after he got up, chased him through Joe Peters's nearby saloon. Price managed to escape but came back later with a pistol and shot Kirby in the leg.

Occasionally, serious affrays occurred at places other than saloons, but oftentimes, alcohol was still involved. On the evening of August 15, 1881, for instance, a man named Edward Holmes, who had been fired from his job at Benjamin Fay's restaurant and boardinghouse in North Springfield, got drunk and returned to his former place of employment in a quarrelsome, boisterous mood. When Fay tried to put him out, Holmes stabbed his former boss in the side with a pocketknife. The wound was considered serious but was not fatal, and Holmes was committed to the county jail.

The saloons, of course, also contributed to general revelry and hell-raising in which no one was injured. On May 4, 1886, the *Leader* reported that "disgraceful proceedings" had been taking place in and around Kern's Office Saloon on South Street every evening for the past month. On the night of May 3, six women had been "carousing around and raising Cain," necessitating the attention of the police until 3:30 in the morning, when the saloon finally closed up. A city ordinance required saloons to shut down at midnight, but according to the newspaper, patrons continued to slip in and out of them after hours.

The number of saloons in Springfield varied over the years, but eight were known to be in operation in 1881. In an issue of the *Patriot-Advertiser* from that year, the paper's editor remarked, "If saloons are institutions to be proud of, then ours should be a proud city." The paper noted that several of the town's saloons were "not common doggeries…They occupy first class business buildings, pay $600.00 a year license, as much more probably for rent, are furnished in gorgeous style, and yet make money. The fact that they can be run on so expensive a scale and still live, shows that they must be liberally patronized."

Two years later, when the county court raised the cost of a liquor license from $150 to $550, the total cost for the privilege of running a saloon in Springfield, including $50 in state fees and $600 in city fees, came to $1,200 a year, and this did not include rent, government taxes or other incidentals. Although the very legality and availability of alcohol remained a controversial issue throughout the 1880s, many Springfieldians supported the increase in licensing fees. Temperance advocates no doubt saw the high costs of maintaining a saloon as an obstacle for saloonkeepers and believed the financial burden would reduce the number of saloons or force that industry to shut down completely. Government officials probably went along with the rise in fees because of the increased revenue generated. Most of the Springfield saloonkeepers, however, seemed unaffected by the increase in license fees. For example, J.M. Kirby, while noting that the increase from $150 to $550 was a "pretty good jump," felt that he could stand the raise as long as the drugstores, which weren't required to pay the liquor licensing fee, were not allowed to skirt the law and become de facto saloons, where people could readily get liquor by "prescription." Kirby, according to the *Patriot*, "spoke in severe terms" about such "drug stores."

In 1887, Missouri passed a "local option" law, which gave individual towns within the state the power to decide whether to allow the sale of liquor in their communities. After a hard-fought campaign in the fall of 1887, the people of Springfield passed a local option ordinance 1,722 to 1,472. However, the law did not stem the flow of alcohol in Springfield for long, if at all. Springfield's local option ordinance remained in effect only a couple of years before it was overturned by an appellate judge.

Gambling operations in Springfield, as elsewhere, tended to be allied with saloons. During the town's very early days, gambling often took place in the saloon itself, and the operation was frequently run by the saloonkeeper. In the late nineteenth century and into the twentieth, however, the gambling setup was more likely located in a connected room, usually a back room or a room upstairs in the same building. Sometimes the operation was still run by the saloonkeeper. In the summer of 1889, for instance, Winkle and Schoner kept a gambling room above their saloon on Boonville, and they sold and cashed the chips themselves. More likely, though, by the 1880s, someone other than the saloonkeeper ran the gambling operation, and often the only direct relationship between the two establishments was the mutual benefit of attracting more customers that each derived from the other. In April 1883, for instance, J.R. Miles was charged with running a poker table in a room above Kern's saloon. The case was prosecuted under the Johnson gambling law, passed in Missouri in 1881, which allowed the offense of running a gambling operation to be classified as a felony. In the Miles case, the defendant's counsel claimed the Johnson law was not intended to apply to poker games, and the defense also cited a lack of sufficient evidence. The charge against Miles was then reduced to a misdemeanor, and the case was tried before a jury. Miles's trial ended in a hung jury, with the six jurors evenly split for conviction and acquittal. Among the witnesses for the prosecution against Miles was Joe Armstrong, who was one of Springfield's most notorious gamblers of the era. No doubt he had been a participant in the poker game and was testifying only because he was compelled to. In addition to his involvement in the Miles case, Armstrong, who listed his occupation as "musician" at the time of the 1880 census, was cited in circuit court numerous times between the years 1886 and 1890 for offenses ranging from mere "gambling" to "permitting a gambling device to be set up and used."

The Black Crook Billiard Hall, one of the more notorious gambling establishments in Springfield, got its start during the 1880s. It was located next door to a saloon on South Alley near Kirby Arcade. When Taylor Smith was called to testify about the Black Crook before a grand jury in 1889, he tried not to incriminate himself but admitted that he "went there occasionally" and saw craps and other gambling games being played during his visits. He said customers could pay their money and "drinks would come in from the barroom in a few minutes." Smith said owner Joe Hailey was always in charge of the money and chips, which cost a nickel apiece, and Hailey sometimes brought the drinks as well. In reality, Smith's connection to the Black Crook involved a good deal more than occasional visits. He, in fact, ran the gambling operation, and the Black Crook was often referred to as "Taylor Smith's place."

Although billiard halls often operated as separate, primary businesses, most saloons also had billiard tables to entertain their customers. In 1882, Constable F.M. Donnell (later sheriff of Greene County) testified before a grand jury that J.C.F. Kinney's, J.M. Kirby's and A.F. Kinney's establishments, as well as the Metropolitan Hotel saloon, each had billiard tables, pool tables and pigeon-hole tables. Donnell explained that each game generally cost twenty cents to play and a player could have a complimentary drink during the game if he wanted. "If not, you pay 20 cents anyway."

Prostitution was also on the rise in the 1880s. Although Belle Wilson was clearly the Cyprian queen of Springfield during the 1880s, as her numerous citations for keeping a bawdyhouse spanned the entire decade, she was not the only peddler of sex in the city. William and Elizabeth Jackson were cited for keeping a bawdyhouse several times between 1880 and 1883. Belle Osborn was indicted in 1885, Lula McLaughlin in 1888 and W.L. Maxwell in 1889. Also in 1889, Tina Smith was indicted for keeping a bawdyhouse at the corner of Phillips and Campbell Streets.

In early April 1883, the "notorious Belle Carson," whom the *Patriot* identified as a prostitute, was implicated in a scandalous rape case in North Springfield that involved her thirteen-year-old sister-in-law. Belle was married to the girl's older brother or had been at one time. However, she had been reportedly keeping company with a married man named Richard Airey. Aided and abetted by her mother-in-law, Belle "procured the deflowering of the child" by her paramour. Airey was subsequently arrested for rape.

A brief item from the *Patriot* in 1883 shows that prostitution was not uncommon in Springfield during the decade. On May 3, 1883, the newspaper reported that eleven men had appeared in court the previous day; four were charged with visiting bawdyhouses, and the remaining seven were brought in for "being plain drunks." Two of the whoremongers were fined eight dollars each plus costs. The other two were fined ten dollars each, one of them because he was also drunk and the other one because he was carrying a pistol at the time of his arrest. The plain drunks were fined three dollars each.

In 1889, during Ralph Walker's second term as mayor of Springfield, a petition that was signed by forty-five citizens was presented to the mayor. The petition stated that a house at 904 East Mill Street, which was known to be "a common bawdyhouse," was a great annoyance to many citizens and requested that the city take the necessary steps to abate the nuisance.

Although prostitution was present in Springfield during the 1880s, it was not as rampant as barroom brawls and saloon murders. But it would only be a few more decades before it reached its peak.

Chapter Six

The Most Scandalous
Murder Case in the History
of Greene County

After the decomposed body of Sarah Graham was found on February 25, 1886, in an abandoned well on the farm of nationally known temperance revivalist Emma Molloy located at the western edge of modern-day Springfield and Sarah's husband, George Graham, was suspected of killing her, the *Springfield Express* called the murder "the most wanton murder ever recorded in the annals of crime." In 1915, local historians Fairbanks and Tuck described the legal proceedings against Ms. Molloy and her foster daughter Cora Lee, who were charged as accessories to the crime, as the "most spectacular court procedure in the entire life of the county." The *Express*'s assessment of the murder in its immediate aftermath was perhaps an exaggeration, but Fairbanks and Tuck's judgment rendered twenty-nine years after the fact still rings true today. If there has ever been a more sensational criminal case in the history of Greene County than the murder of Sarah Graham, including the subsequent vigilante action against her husband and the legal proceedings against Molloy and Lee, this author is unaware of it.

Forty-five-year-old Emma Molloy, whom one newspaper called the most eloquent temperance lecturer in America, came to Springfield in May 1885 to conduct a series of revival meetings at the First Congregational Church in North Springfield. George Graham, a thirty-five-year-old ex-convict whom Mrs. Molloy had befriended several years earlier during her ministry at the Indiana State Prison North, soon followed, arriving in Springfield about June 1 that same year. Graham had been associated with Mrs. Molloy in 1884 in the publication of a temperance newspaper called the *Morning and Day of Reform*. Additionally, Graham, his wife and their two sons shared a house in Washington with Molloy; her fifteen-year-old son, Frank; her eighteen-year-old adopted daughter, Etta; her twenty-four-year-old foster daughter, Cora Lee; and Cora's younger sister, Emma Lee.

In February 1885, Sarah Graham took her sons, thirteen-year-old Charlie and six-year-old Roy, and went back to her father's home at Fort Wayne, Indiana, while George Graham stayed on

One newspaper called Emma Molloy the most eloquent temperance lecturer in America. *Photo from author's collection.*

with the Molloy family. When the *Morning and Day of Reform* folded a couple of months later because of financial difficulties, Mrs. Molloy resumed her temperance lecturing and soon landed in Springfield. Graham, meanwhile, briefly went back to Fort Wayne to attend his father's funeral but continued to correspond with the Molloy family as he traveled about. In mid- to late May, he sent letters to Cora Lee and Emma Molloy from Concordia, Kansas, openly declaring his love for Cora, a passion that had been smoldering for some time. Graham explained that Sarah had divorced him in 1873 shortly after he went to prison on a charge of larceny and that he and Sarah had been living in sin since his release. He begged Cora to forgive him for his transgression and assured her that there was no impediment to keep them apart.

Convinced he was telling the truth, Cora invited him to Springfield, and the romance between them began in earnest when he arrived. They were married on July 18 by the Reverend J.C. Plumb, minister of the First Congregational Church, and arrangements were made for the newlyweds to live with the Molloy family on a farm between Springfield and Brookline, which Judge James Baker had financed for Mrs. Molloy at the close of her revival. A recent convert to the Prohibitionist Party, Baker was a former judge of the Missouri Supreme Court and was considered one of Springfield's leading citizens. George Graham was to act as manager of the farm, which was located just west of Wilson Creek at Farm Road 150 (also known as Old Sunshine Road).

Emma Molloy, who had never held Sarah Graham in high esteem and who hoped that Cora's marriage to Graham might be an ameliorating influence on him, clipped a copy of the marriage notice from a Springfield newspaper and mailed it to Sarah a few weeks after the wedding, unaware that Graham's story to her and Cora was only partially true. George and Sarah had, indeed, divorced in 1873, but he had left out the fact that they had remarried after he got out of prison and had remained married even during his second stint in prison on a forgery conviction during the late 1870s. Outraged when she received the marriage notice, Sarah wrote to Graham demanding to know what was going on, and Graham replied, denying that he and Cora were married. He admitted the truth only after Sarah wrote back enclosing the newspaper clipping, and he proposed to give Sarah money if she would keep her mouth shut and let Charlie and Roy come and stay with him on the Molloy farm. Sarah agreed to meet him in St. Louis with the kids, but it is not known if she ever intended to give them up.

In September, Graham told Cora and Mrs. Molloy that he wanted to go to Fort Wayne to bring the kids back, and Mrs. Molloy, before leaving on a temperance crusade, gave him money to make the trip. Bidding Cora goodbye, Graham left sometime around the end of the month and met Sarah in St. Louis a day later. Graham tried to talk Sarah into returning to Fort Wayne or staying with an uncle in St. Louis, but she insisted on continuing the trip to Springfield. She, Graham and their two boys left St. Louis by train on September 30 and arrived at the North Springfield depot that evening. Graham took his boys to Benjamin Fay's nearby restaurant and boardinghouse to spend the night. His precise movements after that were a matter of lengthy debate at the subsequent legal proceedings against Emma Molloy and Cora Lee, but according to Graham's confession, he and Sarah went to South Town and had dinner. They then walked to the Gulf depot at the corner of Main and Mill Streets, where Graham tried vainly to get Sarah to take a train to Kansas City. (Springfield's second railroad, the Kansas City, Springfield

& Memphis, was often called the Gulf Railroad, and its depot was located closer to the public square than the Commercial Street depot.)

Graham decided to strike out on foot for the Brookline farm, hoping that Sarah surely would not follow him the whole way, but she came right along. When they reached the gate leading to the Molloy farm in the wee hours of October 1, Graham gave his determined first wife one last chance to turn back, but Sarah insisted that she was going to go up to the house and "clear Cora out." According to Graham, he was whittling on a stick with his pocket knife and Sarah had a small limb in her hand, and when he reminded Sarah that she had cheated on him a couple of years earlier, she struck him with the limb. Graham threw up his hand to ward off the blow and accidentally cut Sarah with the knife. The two then began to struggle, and Graham killed her by stabbing her in the neck. After undressing the body, Graham dropped Sarah in an abandoned well located on the Molloy farm about three hundred yards from the house and threw her clothing in after her. He then went back to the main road and walked about one hundred feet west of the house. Making it appear he had come in from the west, the direction of the nearest train depot, he cut across a field to the house and tapped on a window to let Cora know he was home.

The next morning, Graham returned to Springfield to get Charlie and Roy and drove them back to the Molloy farm in a buggy. During the trip, he lied to his sons about their mother's whereabouts and gave them strict instructions that they were to say that they had left her in St. Louis.

Later that fall, Abbie Breese, who had not heard from her sister for some time, became concerned about Sarah's welfare and began writing letters from Fort Wayne inquiring about her whereabouts. At first, Abbie wrote directly to Graham, who told her, as he had told Molloy and Cora Lee, that he had left Sarah in St. Louis and that she had mentioned something about going to see her brother in Washington Territory. Still, Abbie persisted, and Graham finally lost his patience and told her to stop pestering him.

The only significant difference between the story Graham told Abbie and the one he told Molloy and Cora Lee was that he let Molloy and Cora believe he had gone all the way to Fort Wayne to get the boys and Sarah had come part of the way with them when, in fact, he had prearranged to meet her in St. Louis. Following their father's orders, Charlie and Roy corroborated the story that their mother had been left in St. Louis. After receiving a number of letters from Abbie asking about Sarah, Graham suggested to Molloy and Cora that Sarah's family was just trying to make trouble for him with their dogged inquiries.

But Graham wasn't the only one to whom Abbie and her family wrote. Brookline constable W.J. O'Neal received a letter from Sarah and Abbie's father, Marquis Gorham, on Christmas morning in 1885 expressing his suspicion that the family had not been told the truth about Sarah and asking O'Neal to see what he could find out. O'Neal received a second letter of inquiry several days later, and he went out in early January to the Molloy farm but found only Etta Molloy, Emma Lee and the Graham boys at home. Not knowing there were two Mrs. Grahams, the constable asked where Mrs. Graham was and was told she was in Springfield. A few days later, when O'Neal saw George Graham at Brookline, Graham told him Sarah was out at the farm and the reason she didn't write her folks was because she had a sore hand.

As the scrutiny intensified, Graham decided to take off, and he forged checks at three Springfield banks to finance his flight. Telling Cora he was going to look for work, he traveled to Paola, Kansas, where, on January 10, he wrote to Molloy, who was holding a revival at Dunlap, Kansas. He confessed that Sarah was missing and that he had become the object of an investigation into her disappearance but claimed it was all a conspiracy by the Gorham family to ruin him. He also admitted forging the checks. Mrs. Molloy said she would make the checks good and that he should go back home or else his continued absence would make him look guilty. Graham balked but later met Molloy in Kansas City, and she convinced him to go back to Springfield with her.

Meanwhile, Constable O'Neal, who had learned of George Graham's marriage to Cora Lee, stopped by the Molloy farm around January 16 to make further inquiries into Sarah's disappearance. Cora told him she knew nothing about Sarah and asked him to come back on Monday, January 18, when she expected Graham to be home.

Molloy and Graham arrived as scheduled, and Mrs. Molloy promptly went to the Springfield banks to make Graham's forged checks good. On January 20, Charlie Graham returned from Brookline and announced that he had signed a letter to Abbie Breese without reading it, which he had allowed Constable O'Neal to write on his behalf because his hands were too cold. The news threw the Molloy household into a panic. Graham declared that Charlie might have signed his life away by unknowingly implicating him in Sarah's disappearance, and he dispatched Molloy and Cora to Brookline to try to retrieve the letter or learn its contents. The two women promptly drove to Brookline in a buggy and intercepted O'Neal and postmaster John Potter. During the animated discussion that ensued, one of the men demanded to know Sarah's whereabouts, and the women stated that Sarah Graham might be in a house of ill fame in St. Louis. Although not convinced, Potter let the women open the letter and read it. Satisfied that it contained nothing incriminating, they let Potter repost it and then returned home. Shortly afterward, Molloy departed for Peoria, Illinois, for a new revival.

The next week, Abbie Breese and her husband, T.L. Breese, arrived in Springfield, and Mr. Breese swore out a warrant for Graham's arrest on a charge of bigamy. Graham was arrested on January 29 and was lodged in jail at Springfield to await a preliminary hearing.

In the wake of Graham's arrest for bigamy, Springfield newspapers eagerly reported the salacious news, and at least one local daily fanned the flames of scandal by reprinting excerpts from a story that had appeared in the January 21 *Fort Wayne News* after word of Graham's forgeries reached his and Sarah's hometown. "It would seem that the erratic George Graham will never cease while life lasts to furnish newspaper sensations," the Fort Wayne article began. The article detailed the misdeeds that had landed Graham in prison twice and further mentioned that Graham was rumored to have had a liaison with Mrs. Emma Molloy. On January 22, as more information about Sarah Graham's disappearance reached Fort Wayne, the *News* followed up its article with another story further impugning Mrs. Molloy: "Does Mrs. Molloy expect the public forever to excuse the strange incidents that ever and anon mark her career?" the newspaper asked. "What strange infatuation is that which makes this lady write effusive love letters to an ex-convict?"

On February 1, Graham made public the first of a series of missives and statements he would issue from his jail cell. He not only claimed he had nothing to do with Sarah's disappearance and denied the charges of immoral conduct between himself and Mrs. Molloy, but he also suggested that he was not guilty of bigamy. However, proof of Graham's bigamy was presented at his preliminary hearing, which was held on February 4 and 5. Nearly two thousand spectators packed the courthouse, and Graham was afterward returned to jail in default of a $1,000 bond. With Graham securely behind bars, Potter and others called for a thorough search of the Molloy premises. On February 25, Sarah Graham's nude

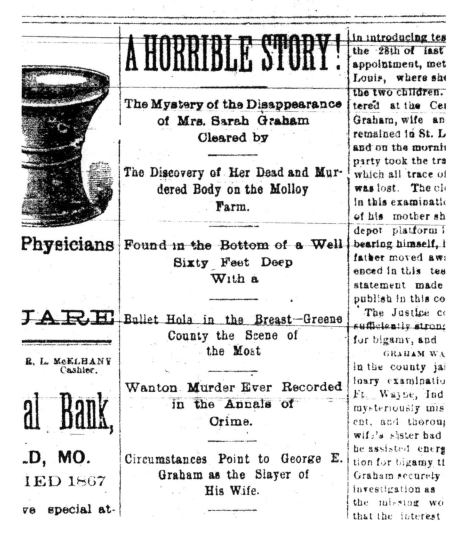

SPRINGFIELD. MO., FRIDAY MORNI

A HORRIBLE STORY!

The Mystery of the Disappearance
of Mrs. Sarah Graham
Cleared by

The Discovery of Her Dead and Murdered Body on the Molloy
Farm.

Found in the Bottom of a Well
Sixty Feet Deep
With a

Bullet Hole in the Breast—Greene
County the Scene of
the Most

Wanton Murder Ever Recorded
in the Annals of
Crime.

Circumstances Point to George E.
Graham as the Slayer of
His Wife.

Physicians

JARH

R. L. McELHANY
Cashier.

al Bank,

_D, MO.

IED 1867

ve special at-

In introducing tes
the 28th of last
appointment, met
Louis, where she
the two children.
tered at the Cel
Graham, wife an
remained in St. L
and on the morni
party took the tra
which all trace of
was lost. The cl
in this examinatio
of his mother sh
depot platform i
bearing himself, i
father moved aw:
enced in this tes
statement made
publish in this co
The Justice co
sufficiently stron;
for bigamy, and
GRAHAM WA
in the county jai
inary examinatio
Ft. Wayne, Ind
mysteriously mis
ent. and thorou;
wife's sister had
be assisted energ
tion for bigamy, th
Graham securely
investigation as
the missing wo
that the interest

Headline from the *Springfield Express* after Sarah Graham's body was discovered.

body was found in the abandoned well on the Molloy farm and brought to Springfield. A coroner's inquest was held the following day, and the examination of witnesses drew a large crowd. At the inquest, Charlie Graham revealed for the first time that he and his brother had been compelled by their father to lie about their mother's whereabouts.

Graham had issued a second statement after his preliminary hearing on the bigamy charge, and he put forth a third while the coroner's inquest was in session. In each case, he told a slightly altered version of his previous story, as new evidence against him continued to emerge.

In early to mid-February, Reverend Plumb had written to Emma Molloy at Peoria urging her to come home to answer the rumors swirling about her name in connection with the Graham case. Molloy arrived in Springfield on Sunday morning, February 28, and was met at the depot by Judge Baker and Sheriff F.M. Donnell. Donnell immediately arrested Molloy and placed her under guard at a deputy's residence as a suspected accessory to Sarah Graham's murder. Cora Lee was also arrested that morning on the same charge. Later the same day, Graham and the two women began an exchange of communications from their respective chambers. There had been talk all weekend of mob violence, and Cora, fearing for her and Emma's lives, sent Graham an impassioned letter beseeching him to tell the truth and save her and Emma. Meanwhile, rumors that Mrs. Molloy had turned against him reached Graham. She had finally admitted that he was more than likely guilty of the crime he had been accused of and was reportedly plotting against him with Judge Baker. Graham fired off a short letter to Molloy warning her not to exhibit her "feline qualities" toward him.

The next day, however, perhaps in response to Cora's entreaties, Graham prepared a full and lengthy confession detailing the events leading up to Sarah's murder and taking sole responsibility for the deed. He said Molloy and Cora neither participated in the crime nor had any knowledge of it, and he insisted that the murder weapon had been a knife. Later that day, March 1, the jury returned a contrary verdict that Sarah Graham came to her death by means of a gunshot wound to the breast at the hands of George Graham and that Cora Lee and Emma Molloy were accessories. Molloy wrote to Graham on March 2, addressing him as "my poor boy." She said she was praying for him and denied the rumors he had heard that she and Judge Baker were "trying to close [his] mouth by mob violence." A funeral service was held the next day for Sarah Graham, and her remains were afterward interred at Maple Park Cemetery. The same day, Molloy and Cora Lee were moved to the Polk County jail at Bolivar while they awaited their preliminary hearings.

In early March, several anonymous letters alternately supporting and denouncing the twice-divorced Molloy appeared in several Springfield

Sarah Graham's headstone at Maple Park Cemetery. *Photo by author.*

newspapers as well as others. A letter from Washington, Kansas, was especially critical, accusing Molloy of carrying on an adulterous affair with Graham while the two families lived in the same house at that town. Another letter labeled Graham a liar and said Mrs. Molloy was being crucified merely for being his guardian angel for the past few years. Graham issued a rebuttal, claiming that he had been an equal partner in all his enterprises with Mrs. Molloy. He also renewed his warning that neither she nor Cora should say anything to encourage attacks on him.

The preliminary hearing for Emma Molloy and Cora Lee began on March 12, and throngs of people packed the courthouse for each day's session. Among the most damning evidence offered by the prosecution was the discrepancy between the verdict of the coroner's jury that Sarah Graham had been killed by gunshot and George's insistence that he had killed her with a knife. The prosecution's argument was that Cora had been in on the killing or accomplished it on her own and that Graham was simply trying to protect her. It's plausible, however, that he might simply have been trying to make his crime appear less premeditated than it was. Seeking to establish Cora's movements during the hours leading up to the murder, the prosecution also introduced several witnesses who claimed to have seen her on the night in question, although some of the testimony was contradictory. The most scandalous testimony was offered by Charlie Graham, who said that before his father married Cora Lee, he had seen his dad in bed with either Cora Lee or Emma Molloy at various places, including Washington, Kansas. He added that, on at least one occasion, he had seen all three of them in bed together at the same time.

On March 16, a few days after the preliminary hearing opened, Graham wrote a letter to Cora warning her to tell not just the truth but the *whole* truth. However, Graham suspected Cora and Molloy were plotting against him, and on March 20, he issued a detailed statement chronicling his relationship (sexual or otherwise) with both women from the time he met them. He said that he first became associated with Molloy in the publication of the *Morning and Day of Reform* in early 1882, shortly after her divorce from her second husband and before he and Sarah had reconciled. After working closely with Molloy for several months, he declared his love for her on November 17, 1882, at Elgin, Illinois. Although she protested mildly at first, the two shared their first moment of "criminal intimacy" two days later at Molloy's house. According to Graham, he first had sex with Cora Lee on January 4, 1883, and he continued to make love to both women on a more or less regular basis after that until his marriage to Cora. His statement disclosed specific dates, places and other circumstances of many of the liaisons and even included the initials of doctors who had supposedly performed abortions for one or both women.

The long preliminary hearing finally ended on March 31. Cora Lee was charged with being an accessory before the fact, and the court ordered that she be held without bail until her trial in May. Emma Molloy was charged with being an accessory after the fact and was held on a $5,000 bond, which she promptly paid with the help of several prominent Springfield citizens who acted as sureties. A week and a half later, Judge Baker, who was Mrs. Molloy's principal surety and who had come under criticism for helping her, offered a detailed statement on why he continued to support her. In the statement, he refuted, point by point, many of the accusations against her. Shortly afterward, Cora Lee was granted bail, and he helped secure her bond as well.

In the wee morning hours of April 27, while George Graham was still awaiting his preliminary hearing on the murder charge, a large body of men rode up College Street to the jail at the corner of the public square, broke into the prisoner's cell, took him to a spot on West Linn Street not far from present-day Grant Beach Park and hanged him from a tree. The mob apparently feared Graham might be granted a continuance or a change of venue. A note was pinned to Graham's body warning other potential murderers to steer clear of Greene County. It also cautioned

Sheriff Donnell to keep his mouth shut should he recognize any of the men involved in the lynching. The note was inscribed to "the memory of Sarah Graham…whose life was sacrificed at the altar of Hecate," and it was signed "The Three Hundred."

Moments before George Graham was about to be hanged, he reportedly issued a final declaration that he and he alone was guilty of killing Sarah. Apparently anticipating the possibility of his lynching, he had also left several notes in his jail cell addressed to his children, Cora and Greene County officials, respectively. In the letter to his children, he wrote that Cora loved them and that she was innocent of the crime she had been accused of. In his letter to Cora, he suggested that the case against him was a "put up affair," and he signed it "your ever loving, faithful husband." His letter to county officials reaffirmed the complete innocence of Cora Lee and Emma Molloy in Sarah's murder.

In mid-May, Emma Molloy wrote a long letter to the public that was published in the *Springfield Express* and other papers, in which she again said she was innocent, not only of being an accessory to Sarah Graham's murder but also of the sexual indiscretions Graham had accused her of. She even offered evidence, such as documents she had signed at certain places and the testimony of multiple eyewitnesses, proving that she could not possibly have been where Graham said she was on many of the occasions detailed in his account of their affair. She attributed much of the scandal surrounding her to the fact that she was not only a revivalist but also female: "There are no two classes of people whom the world…so readily believe a scandal about as a minister of the gospel and a woman, but when the two characters are combined, and a scandal can be concocted sufficiently ingenious for the public to swallow, however nauseating and polluting it may be, it is devoured with an ecstasy of delight." Critics, however, pointed out that she had waited until after Graham was dead to rebut his charges.

While still suffering the disgrace of the Graham scandal, Molloy, who had lost two children early in her first marriage, saw her life struck by tragedy yet again when Frank, her only surviving biological child, drowned at Pine Lake in Indiana. A couple of months later, she herself almost drowned when she threw herself into a river in what was perhaps a suicide attempt, and she had to be rescued.

Cora Lee finally went on trial in 1887, at which time the *New York Times* referred to the Graham murder as "one of the most shocking crimes ever committed in the West." Cora testified in her own defense, and Emma Molloy traveled to Springfield from Washington Territory, where she was working to reestablish her reputation as a temperance revivalist, to testify. Perhaps the two key witnesses for the defense, however, were Cora's sisters, Etta Molloy and Emma Lee, both of whom never wavered from their testimony that Cora Lee had been at home with them all evening on the night of Sarah's murder. In addition, people who had known Cora while she lived in Indiana submitted numerous affidavits swearing to her outstanding character. The trial ended in a hung jury, with eight jurors voting for conviction and four for acquittal. Shortly afterward, Emma Molloy was granted a change of venue to Christian County in her case.

Cora was re-tried in 1888 and acquitted, and the case against Emma Molloy was subsequently dropped. However, the Sarah Graham murder case remained a subject of controversy and debate for some years afterward. The author of the *Pictorial and Genealogical Record of Greene County* (1893), for instance, praised Judge Baker for his "courageous defense of Mrs. Malloy [*sic*], who was persecuted because she was a temperance advocate by the worst saloon element in Springfield." Even today, though, 125 years after the fact, there are those familiar with the Graham case who take an opposite view, believing that Baker was guilty of orchestrating the lynching of George Graham to shut him up so that he wouldn't further incriminate Emma Molloy.

Perhaps the only two things that can be said about Mrs. Molloy's involvement in the Graham case is that she was, at the very least, guilty of poor judgment and gullibility. In the first instance, she was guilty for trusting a man who had repeatedly proved himself unworthy of trust; in the second, she was naïve enough to believe his web of lies even after he had betrayed her by writing bad checks and evidence began to point to him as his wife's likely killer. As for Cora Lee, suffice it to say that, if she had been charged with being an accessory after the fact instead of before the fact, the outcome in her case might have been different. Still, there is room for reasonable doubt.

Chapter Seven

The Naughty Nineties

Despite having been charged with keeping a bawdyhouse in 1889, Belle Wilson continued to be a Springfield madam. In the early to mid-1890s, she and Rosa Jones ran a brothel at 895 Franklin Street in a house Belle rented from Martha Misner (also known as Martha Bush). In 1890, Norville Milligan told an investigating jury that he and four other young men had recently called at Madam Belle's place and that he and one of the other men had gone upstairs with two of the several girls who stayed there. The girls who were not busy with Norville and his friend tried to get the other men to go upstairs, too, but they declined the invitation. Norville testified that he paid Belle three dollars for a half hour's worth of upstairs entertainment.

In 1894, two of Belle's girls, Grace Lee and Nellie Gray, were called before a grand jury, and they admitted that they "led a sporting life." They testified that they always gave half of their earnings to Rosa and each usually paid a fine of $9.15 a month.

In early 1895, Martha Misner moved into Springfield from an outlying farm and started her own "sporting business" in some rooms over a store on Campbell Street near its intersection with College Street. In March, police raided the place and arrested two girls and two men who were in bed together.

About the same time, Belle Wilson vacated Martha's house on Franklin Street, and the sixty-nine-year-old landlady took charge of it. A policeman stopped by the bordello to levy fines against Martha, and she reportedly told him that she couldn't afford to let the brothel stand idle and that "this is the only way I can get any income from it."

Shortly afterward, a man named Hindman told a grand jury that Mrs. Misner, to the best of his knowledge, was the only person in town running a bawdyhouse. Martha had become the empress of Springfield madams, but it's unlikely her bagnio was the only one in Springfield, as Mr. Hindman claimed. A few months after he testified before the grand jury, the *Springfield Leader-Democrat* reported, "The city is overrun with immoral women and girls." According to the article, the town jail at the time was so filthy and overcrowded that it was considered inhumane "to confine the women in this hole." In most instances, the women who were hauled into court on moral charges simply paid fines of five dollars (as well as court costs) and were then let go. The problem, however, was

Photograph of the Springfield calaboose. *Photo by author.*

that "the more brazen and hardened ones" were the ones with the most money, while the more innocent, young girls who were "just starting in a life of immorality" had difficulties paying their fines.

By way of illustration, a reporter for the *Leader-Democrat* told the story of an unfortunate young girl named Myrtle Miller who, after visiting her aunt at Clinton, had arrived back in Springfield on her way to her home several miles outside town. With plans to continue the journey the next day, she stayed overnight with an acquaintance who lived in a house that turned out to be a questionable resort occupied by a number of fancy women. The place was raided by police on the night Myrtle arrived, and she was arrested, hauled into court along with the rest of the inmates and fined the same as they were. Among the young women appearing before the judge with Myrtle was Cora Arnold, who had a record of "lewd and lascivious conduct" that stretched back to 1891. The judge made a special dispensation in Myrtle's case and allowed her to go home until she could pay the fine. Although Myrtle was apparently an innocent girl who was merely in the wrong place at the wrong time, both the judge and the newspaperman seemed unconvinced, as the article added that the judge allowed her to go home "provided her parents wanted her to come."

The *Leader-Democrat* reporter concluded, "Wichita, Clinton, Sedalia and other towns seem to be driving out their dissolute women. Over the past few days, droves of them from those places have arrived in this city. The police promise to keep the court busy for a week to come unless the women conclude to go on to other fields. Not less than 50 of the women have arrived in this city recently and this number added to the home supply makes the number entirely too large."

In November 1895, Grant Brown added further evidence suggesting that Mr. Hindman had underestimated the breadth of prostitution in Springfield. Brown testified that he knew Jane Dills and a woman named Mrs. Crawford ran a bawdyhouse in Springfield because he had been there himself and had "seen Bill Love, Monroe Hill, Matt Gray, and myself there."

In March 1898, Annie Brownfield was the subject of a grand jury investigation for reportedly running a house of ill repute at 479 West Commercial. Located at the corner of Lyon Street, this house may well have been the same one Martha Wallace and Belle Wilson had occupied. Jennie Barclay, who stayed at the house during January 1898, told the jury, "Mrs. Brownfield is a woman of bad repute. Miss Clara Belle, also of bad repute, boarded at the same place." Barclay also said that men frequently called at the house and that Mrs. Brownfield would take them into a back room for an hour, sometimes two hours. Nellie Neece, who lived next door to the Brownfield house, substantiated Barclay's claims, saying, "I should call her house a sporting house. She had three or four girls there with her and men kept coming there night and day."

Twenty-two-year-old Laura Thompson, who was staying at the Brownfield house at the time of the investigation, told the jury that Annie had fled to St. Louis after learning an inquiry was underway. Laura said she had seen various men and women in bed together at Annie's house. She testified that she had seen Annie's thirteen-year-old daughter, as well as Annie, in bed with men and, on one occasion, had even seen Annie and her daughter in bed together with the same man. Although Laura claimed to have recently arrived in Springfield from Joplin, a man named Tony Arnold swore he had seen her at another Springfield bawdyhouse several months earlier.

Cassie Stone made her first appearance in Greene County court records when a grand jury investigated her and three other girls who lived together on Jefferson Street in 1896 for possible prostitution. Cassie claimed she was a dressmaker and that her record was spotless; she had even kicked one of the other girls out of the house because of the girl's questionable conduct. In 1898, however, when Cassie was again called before a grand jury, she made little pretense of being anything other than a sporting girl. She testified that she and the other girls had been paying fines of $6.65 on a regular basis "almost every month for the past year" to the city marshal, William Bishop, and that she and the others had never had to go to court. The following year, however, Cassie did appear in court, where she was found guilty of keeping a bawdyhouse and was assessed a much steeper penalty of $200.

In 1899, Martha Misner's "boardinghouse" at 897 North Franklin Avenue, sometimes called the Plain View Hotel or the White House, was still going strong. Two of the parlor girls who stayed with her were Maud Andella and Rosa Cameron (perhaps the same Rosa who had gone by the surname Jones while helping Belle Wilson). When the girls were brought before a grand jury, Rosa boldly stated, "This house is kept as a house of prostitution." She explained that she rented rooms to the men who called at the house and charged them $1.00 for a short term. Reflecting the prior testimony of Cassie Stone, both Rosa and Maud testified that they had paid fines of $6.65 to Springfield officers Armstrong and Baldwin on more than one occasion, and Rosa said the charges against her were always dropped as soon as she paid the fines. It seems that in addition to prostitution, Springfield also had its share of corrupt police officers,

During the prim and proper Victorian era, of course, young women were sometimes wrongly characterized as prostitutes for any act of immorality. Any hint of impropriety or sexual indiscretion, even if it did not involve entertaining strange men for pay, was sure to earn a woman public censure. For instance, Vesta Rider and Mary Clyde, two sixteen-year-old girls, were brought before a grand jury in August 1895 after they were found in William Ferneau's room in the Headley Block at 302–306 Boonville Street with a young man named Charlie Hirsch. A brief investigation revealed that Vesta had been staying with Ferneau and that he had talked her into luring Mary up to his room so that he could "do business with her." Mary admitted that she went to his room and let him kiss and fondle her, but she refused to go to bed with him. She, however, did have intercourse with Hirsch on two separate occasions.

Ferneau was indicted for "lewd and lascivious conduct," specifically for enticing Mary Clyde to his room for immoral purposes, and was bound over to appear before a judge. The *Leader-Democrat* reported that the judge considered Vesta Rider "very dangerous, as he thinks she makes a business of procuring girls. Vesta Rider, being young herself, can gain the confidence of young girls much more easy than a woman can."

Although somewhat more promiscuous than Mary, Vesta, if her grand jury testimony is to be believed, was scarcely the hardened prostitute that the newspaper and the judge made her out to be. Vesta said an older man named Harry Maxwell had brought her to Springfield from Humansville a few months earlier with the promise that he would take her to St. Louis to stay with his sister. According to Vesta, they had registered at a boardinghouse in Springfield as J.H. Maxwell and niece. She had sex with Maxwell in May, and according to her, that was the first time she had ever had intercourse. She met Ferneau on the Fourth of July near the intersection of Boonville and the public square and later had sex with one other man before she started staying with Ferneau. After their appearance before the grand jury, Vesta Rider was taken to the Industrial Home for Girls, and Mary Clyde, who lived in Springfield, was taken home and turned over to her parents.

Prostitution or other immoral sexual conduct was enough of a problem in Springfield during the late 1890s that the revised ordinances of 1897 addressed the issue in detail. Anyone keeping a brothel or house of assignation was subject to a minimum fine of $200 and a maximum of $1,000. Occupants of such houses, meanwhile, were only fined between $1 and $50. In addition, "no prostitute, courtesan or lewd woman" was allowed to "ply her vocation" on the street.

By the 1890s, liquor violations were so common in Springfield that it would be infeasible to enumerate even half of them. However, some of the usual suspects from previous decades still showed up as frequent offenders. James Kirby was cited several

Photograph of a Springfield woman of questionable virtue, circa 1900. *Courtesy Greene County Archives and Records Center.*

times for selling liquor to minors and staying open on Sunday, and apparently, he wasn't pleased by the continual police harassment. He complained to police officer Matt Sims in the fall of 1898 that the police chief had been paid "to let up on the saloon men," but Sims, in relaying the statement to a grand jury, claimed he didn't know of anyone who had gotten any of the "slush money."

Chris Rule, who ran a saloon on Commercial Street near Robberson Avenue, had a log of liquor violations dating back to the late 1870s, and he continued to add to the record during the nineties. Like Kirby's place and all the other saloons, Rule's joint was a frequent target of investigation for liquor violations. In November 1899, for instance, a man named Cunningham told a grand jury that he was "in Chris Rule's saloon on Sunday one or two weeks ago," and he and his companion "got a drink of whiskey."

Indeed, by the 1890s, stopping the sale of liquor on Sunday and preventing its sale to minors had become the primary focus of authorities in dealing with the alcohol issue. In previous decades, citizen-led efforts had concentrated on trying to stop the sale of liquor altogether, while police focused on apprehending those who sold liquor without a license. Although it's likely some temperance crusaders knew that halting the flow of alcohol was going to take years to achieve, it didn't mean they had to let it corrupt their youth or profane their holy day. In November 1897, Dr. C.C. Woods, pastor of St. Paul's Methodist Episcopal Church, told a grand jury that an acquaintance of his who had been in downtown Springfield on a recent Sunday night counted eight saloons that were open and doing business. An arcade where at least one of the saloons was located was so crowded that the man "thought at first there was fight or something of that sort going on."

Other saloonkeepers during the nineties besides Kirby and Rule included Charles and Ike Altschul at the Kentucky Liquor House on the corner of College and Campbell Streets; Joe Peters in William Potter's old place at the corner of Boonville Street and Phelps Avenue; Mac Brooks on College Street and later 428 East Commercial Street; Ed Brooks at 338 East Commercial Street; J.P. Kinsella at 428 East Commercial Street and, later, at the Ozark Hotel on the corner of Benton Avenue and Commercial Street; and Pat Gillespie at the Gulf Saloon, which was located at the corner of Main and Mill Streets near the Gulf depot. All were frequent violators of the liquor laws.

Gambling rolled on in Springfield during the 1890s. As had been the case in the past, most of the gaming was at least loosely associated with saloons. In August 1892, William Bishop and another officer broke up a poker game in a room over Cody and Brooks's saloon on Commercial Street. Among the players who were arrested was one named Kid Elliott. Later that year, Kid was spotted playing poker and craps in the basement under the Metropolitan Hotel saloon, located in the 300 block of West College.

In November 1892, Tom Davidson was indicted for running a gambling house over a saloon kept by the Fisher brothers at the corner of Boonville and Commercial Streets after several men testified to having witnessed gambling on the premises. One of the witnesses said he "saw both of the Fisher brothers shooting craps and saw the fat one cash his checks with Tom Davidson."

In early 1895, Taylor Smith still had charge of the Black Crook, but he had moved the billiard hall to some upstairs rooms at 223 East Olive Street over the Mint Saloon, which was run by Sam Armstrong. Ed Drew helped out at both places, and a man called "Lightning" sometimes handled the gambling games at the Black Crook. There was a stairway leading from the saloon to the gambling hall above and a door separating the two rooms. The door was usually unlocked, but sometimes it was locked when the sporting men wanted to keep out unwelcome visitors. When Smith, Armstrong and Drew were indicted for gambling in March of 1895, Lightning, who was apparently too fast to be taken, eluded arrest.

In November 1895, Sam Greathouse, a noted North Town high roller who had a string of gambling indictments dating back to the mid-1880s, was accused of "playing poker for profit" with several other men in an upstairs room over Kinsella and Grier's saloon, where he was a bartender. Although gambling often took place in or above saloons, gamesters themselves weren't too choosy about where they played, as long as it offered privacy. About the same time as the poker game over Kinsella and Grier's saloon, several men were caught gambling in a vacant boxcar at the Frisco tracks on the north side, which was still often called North Springfield even though it had merged with Springfield several years earlier.

By 1895, gambling, like other vices, was often subject to police corruption. In November, witness A.H. Owings told a grand jury that he knew people were being fined for gambling but that the money was not being accounted for in the Greene County books.

By early 1898, Taylor Smith was no longer associated with the Black Crook, but Sam Armstrong was still on the scene. Lou Huddleston told a grand jury in March that he had "been in the place a dozen times and seen men playing poker and shaking dice for money." The Kentucky Club House was a private men's club located on Olive Street that was also a well-known gambling spot. In March 1899, S.S. Vaughan, a janitor at the club, testified before a grand jury that there was a room in the house known as the "card room or poker room" and that men often played cards with chips at tables set up in this room. Ernest Scholten, nephew of Henry and Emanuel Scholten, was a member of the club, and he testified that alcoholic drinks could be had at the club on Sunday just like any other day, "except that on Sunday payment is made by card." Presumably, members purchased a card ahead of time so that the club could swear, at least somewhat truthfully, that no liquor was "sold" on Sunday.

Chapter Eight

The Aughts and the Ought Nots

C ases involving the rape, seduction or exploitation of girls in their early teens were not uncommon in Springfield one hundred years ago or more just as they are not uncommon nowadays. For instance, in early 1900, Monroe Hill and Sam Hughston were charged with enticing underage girls for immoral purposes after the two men were found drinking in a store building on North Broad Street (now Broadway) with four half-naked young girls.

Probably the main difference between then and now is that back then, offenders in such cases were more likely to get off with light sentences or to escape punishment altogether than they normally would today. Most of the offenders were men, and in a male-controlled world where females were treated as second-class citizens and also held to a higher standard of morality than men, it was often hard to convict a man of a sexual crime. The charges against Hill and Hughston, for instance, were dropped (or so records indicate), although Hill was later sent to prison on a larceny conviction. It should probably be pointed out, too, that a century ago, thirteen-, fourteen- and fifteen-year-old girls were eligible for marriage and, therefore, considered full-grown women.

Women, on occasion, had a hand in the sexual abuse of young females. For example, fourteen-year-old Maud Gouty told a grand jury in July 1900 that George Tackett had come to live with her and her mother in November of the previous year and started sleeping with her mother. Later, her mother told Maud that if George "wanted to do anything to

[her] or have sexual intercourse with [her], for [her] to let him do it." That night George got in bed with Maud, but she still wouldn't let him have sex with her. Her mother told her that George would be angry and "cursing around" if she didn't let him do it. Finally, Maud allowed him to have sex with her, and she told the jury that she had had intercourse with George "lots of times" since then, because he "slept with my mother a while and then slept with me a part of the time."

The story of Mary Stepp, charged in Greene County in late 1900 with keeping a girl under eighteen in a bawdyhouse, provides a more detailed case study of an older woman's exploitation of a girl. Lizzie Rice left her home outside Rogersville in Christian County when she was not quite fourteen years old and came to Springfield in May 1899. In July 1900, after spending a year moving from place to place and working at odd jobs, Lizzie landed at Mollie Young's home on North Cleveland Avenue. Using the alias Clara Brown, she stayed with Mrs. Young for just a couple of weeks before coming down with the mumps. Sometime around August 1, one of Young's neighbors, Mary Stepp, asked Clara to come and stay at her house. Thirty-nine-year-old Mary, who was recently divorced and living with her nine-year-old daughter, told Lizzie she would treat her disease and that Lizzie wouldn't have to work for her room and board.

Lizzie, according to her later testimony, accepted Mary's offer but had no idea "what kind of a house she kept." Not long after Lizzie moved in, Mary had a talk with her and explained "about her way of getting a living and [said] that I had to do as she done." During the two and a half months she lived with Mary, Lizzie "cohabitated" with different men. "The money I got from the men," she said, "I had to divide with Mrs. Stepp." Lizzie said she also saw Mary in bed with several different men during the time she lived with her.

In addition, Lizzie testified that Mary took her around town from saloon to saloon and that every time she was at the Gulf Saloon, she bought beer and whiskey from bartender Red Hall or proprietor Ed Brooks, who had vacated his Commercial Street establishment to take over the Gulf. She said she saw gambling going on in the Wine Room at the Gulf Saloon and that there was also a back room in the place where Brooks allowed those "who spent their money with him" to "do business," and that included Mary Stepp.

A week or so after Mary took Lizzie in, they moved from Cleveland Avenue to some rooms on Patton Alley. Another week or two later, they visited their old neighborhood, and Mary told Mollie Young they were going to have to move again, this time to 302 East Phelps Avenue. She asked Mrs. Young whether or not she knew Lizzie's real name and that she was only fifteen years old. According to Mrs. Young, Mary said that, when the girl came to her house, "she was so green she would only charge 25 cents, and now she had her trained so she would charge $5.00."

Apparently worried about the girl's well-being, Mrs. Young's husband informed policeman H.H. Snow that Lizzie was living with Mary Stepp and suggested that the officer notify the girl's father. When Snow later visited Mary at the Phelps Avenue house, she claimed, according to Snow's written statement to a grand jury, that Lizzie was eighteen years old, didn't have a father and was "a G--Dam hore [*sic*]" from Joplin. Snow warned Mary that the girl was only fourteen or fifteen and that she ought to send her home, but Mary continued to let the girl stay with her.

A month or so later, after determining that the girl was still entertaining men at Mary's house, Snow and another officer arrested both the woman and the girl and put them in the lockup. In the meantime, the police chief had notified the girl's father that Officer Snow wanted to talk to him about his daughter, and Mr. Rice made the trip from Christian County to Springfield. Learning that Lizzie was in the calaboose, he paid her a visit and was allowed to take her home.

Mary Stepp, meanwhile, was accused of keeping an underage girl in a bawdyhouse. Testifying before the grand jury in her own defense, Mary claimed that Lizzie was "a sporting girl" before Mary took her in and that she had a "dose" of venereal disease, not mumps, when she came to live with her. She said that Lizzie and a girl named Emma Hodge had earlier gone to Jasper County and had run around the mining towns of that area, including Webb City and Galena, Kansas, and that the two had "put up a while at a sporting house at Joplin called the Red Onion." Lizzie had supposedly been arrested at a house of ill fame at Carthage and put in jail and was still wanted there on a prostitution charge. Mary then, in what was perhaps an attempt to redeem herself and earn a lighter sentence, named a number of Springfield prostitutes. She said Ella Isley and a girl who lived with Ella in the house next door to Mary on Phelps Avenue were strumpets and that several houses across the street were also occupied by sporting women, including Alice Matlock, Mary Nelson, Mary Bridges, Gabby Harris, Bertie Burns and Sallie Doughbelly. Mrs. Tyner, who lived on nearby Robberson Avenue, was also "a sport."

Mary added that a man named L.A. Cully rented eight houses in her old neighborhood on Cleveland Avenue to sporting women, including Emma Patterson, Mrs. Dill, Becca Dodson, Florence Scott, Lou Wilson and a mother-daughter team of Mrs. Matterson and sixteen-year-old Bessie Matterson. Mary said Cully "knew what kind of women they were" before he rented his houses to them and that he "took part of his rent from some of these women in trade." Mary also said that Mollie Young "keeps two girls," insinuating that Mrs. Young was a madam herself.

Mary explained how she and presumably some of the other sporting women of Springfield operated. She often met men at saloons and would either take them back to her house or to a hotel room. Mary's favorite assignation spot was the Waddle Hotel at 304 South Campbell Street, which was run by Charles Afflack. Mary said, "Whenever a man wants a girl or a woman to go to a room with him, he says 'Let's go to the Afflack house.'" On one occasion, Mary was at the Waddle Hotel with a man at the same time that Belle Chrisman, a fellow prostitute, occupied a nearby room with another man. As part of her testimony, Mary reported that a third man, Fenton Cox, who was in cahoots with Belle, hid under the bed while Belle's john paid her five dollars and undressed. While Belle "raised a racket with the man in bed with her," Cox went through the man's clothes, found several hundred dollars and got out of the room with the money without being seen or heard.

Joe Peters's saloon and the Gulf Saloon were two of Mary's favorite hangouts, and she testified that she knew Peters's saloon hosted gambling and that both places served alcohol to minors. She also named several underage white girls whom she had seen drinking and cavorting with black men at the Gulf Saloon. The litany of state's evidence that Mary provided, however, did her little good. She was formally charged in December 1900 with keeping a girl under eighteen in a bawdyhouse. She was convicted in 1901 and sent to state prison for two years.

Charlie Harper, who testified in the Mary Stepp case, provided a detailed picture of the gambling operation over Joe Peters's saloon. Ed Drew, who had worked at the Black Crook a few years earlier, was running the operation, and Charlie worked for him part time. Gambling in the three upstairs rooms mostly took the form of card playing, usually poker or seven up, and the players always used chips. Two red chips represented a quarter and two whites represented a nickel, while blues were a nickel apiece. Charlie said he often played himself and that he had played with many different men, both black and white, but that women were not allowed in the place. He confirmed a story Mary had told the jury that he once borrowed a dollar from her to go gambling at Ed Drew's place, but he didn't know whether he had won fifty dollars that particular time as she had claimed since he had won fifty dollars so many other times. He further claimed that gambling went on at Drew's place day and night and that there was a door on Phelps Avenue that was kept locked most of the time leading upstairs where the games were held. Inside the door was a small vestibule with a second door opening to the stairway. The second door was always kept locked, but there was a bell on the outside door that men who wanted to gamble could ring. A doorkeeper was usually stationed near the top of the stairs, and when the bell rang, he would go down and let the person in, unless the caller turned out to be a police officer or any other unwelcome visitor.

Additional testimony substantiated Charlie Harper's description of Ed Drew's gambling operation. Men who wanted to gamble in the place bought their chips at the door, and they weren't allowed in if they didn't buy chips. Shooting craps, as well as playing cards, was a common activity, and players rolled the dice on "a big blue table." Real money was occasionally used to play craps, and card players sometimes gambled on pitch, in addition to poker and seven up. Drew was still running the place in early 1901, but his assistants apparently came and went with some regularity. By March, Bob Cain and Charles Cross were helping with the operation, and Charlie Harper was nowhere to be found.

Just as Mary Stepp had impugned virtually every working girl she knew, so, too, did the gamblers often accuse each other. Appearing before a 1901 grand jury, Richard "Sandy" Blakey identified Charles Cross as one of the men who ran Drew's gambling house, but Cross, in turn, told the same jury that Blakey was one of the biggest gamblers in the joint.

William Story told the jury that he owned the building where Peters's saloon was located. He leased the lower part to the Springfield Brewery Company through the company's bookkeeper, Charles Rule, and the brewery in turn rented it to Peters. Story said he rented the upper part to Ed Drew because Rule, son of Commercial Street saloonkeeper Chris Rule, told him that having Drew upstairs "was a benefit to the saloon."

In March 1901, Ed Brooks, whose saloon Mary Stepp and Lizzie Rice had mentioned prominently in their testimony the previous fall, was indicted for keeping a bawdyhouse at his Gulf Saloon. William Cain told the jury that he had gone to the saloon and asked if he could go upstairs, but Brooks told him he couldn't unless he had a woman. If he had a woman, he could get a room for twenty-five cents.

Mac Brooks, like Ed Brooks, had moved from Commercial Street to the south side by 1901. Mac was back on College Street, this time at the Metropolitan Hotel saloon, and he was indicted numerous times in the early 1900s for liquor violations. He was also investigated several times for gambling. Near the end of March 1901, Charles Weaver told a grand jury that he knew of a gambling room behind the billiard hall at the Metropolitan saloon and that Mac Brooks had charge of it. Putting up a puny defense, Brooks told the jury a few days later that he knew of no gambling at the Metropolitan saloon since the beginning of the year except for what "I was interested in myself."

In 1901, the upstairs gambling rooms at 223 East Olive that had previously been known as the Black Crook were now run by Andy Greenstreet. One man told a grand jury that he knew Andy was almost always up there but that he didn't know of any gambling that went on in the rooms. Another witness, Clyde Anderson, offered more damning testimony. He said he had been up there and seen men playing cards with chips. The place consisted of four rooms. One of the rooms had a long table in it, while the other three had small round tables. Andy Greenstreet "had the keys and opened the drawers," Anderson testified. "I seen him unlock the drawers in his dresser and bring out the cards. He seemed to be running the thing."

Several saloons in downtown Springfield around the turn of the twentieth century had slot machines. In 1901, an upstairs room near the Antique Saloon in the Baker Arcade at the northwest corner of the square hosted gambling of all sorts, and the saloon itself sported a nickel slot machine. J.M. Kirby's old saloon in the Kirby Arcade, now run by Cardwell and Jenkins, also had a slot machine. Below the saloon was a ten-pin alley, and customers could push a button and have drinks brought to them from the saloon while they were bowling. Above the saloon was Vint Bray's gambling room, and again, the sporting men could push a button and drinks would come up a chute. During an investigation of Cardwell and Jenkins's business, Kirby told the jury that he owned the building where the saloon was located. In addition to renting the saloon to Cardwell and Jenkins, he also rented one of the upstairs rooms to Vint Bray but on the condition that it not be used for gambling.

Although most gambling in Springfield was associated with saloons, other businesses occasionally fronted minor gambling operations. In late 1901, F.D. Blackburn ran a cigar stand at 310 College Street, but the back room, which was partitioned off from the front by the cigar case and some curtains, was reserved for playing cards. Two or three tables with chairs were set up in the back room, and chips were kept back there in a box. Hearts was the most frequent game played. Each player normally bet ten cents, and the winner raked in all the dimes at the end of the game. In addition, the loser was expected to buy cigars from Mr. Blackburn for all the participants. "It is understood by the players who frequent this place," W.H. Rosenow explained to a grand jury that was investigating the operation, "that someone connected with the games must buy cigars as a consideration for the use of the room."

After the St. Louis–San Francisco Railroad (usually called the Frisco) bought the Gulf Railroad in 1901 and consolidated the two lines into a single passenger depot at the old Gulf location at Main and Mill Streets, the hotel industry, which had previously been centered along Commercial Street, steadily shifted to the vicinity of the new Frisco station. Hotels and rooming houses thrived along College and other nearby streets, and the area west of the square, catering to travelers on the Frisco Railroad, gradually became the hub of Springfield vice.

Rumors circulated in 1902 that the Denton Hotel at 216 North Campbell was secretly being used as an assignation house by some of Springfield's red-light ladies, but porter Jack Coleman told the grand jury, "I am acquainted with a good many of the prostitutes around town, and I know that none of them have been taking their meals or rooming at the Denton." Chambermaid Vina Green was not so unequivocal. She claimed that while she had no personal knowledge of such seedy activity at the Denton, she knew several women had been put out of the hotel for allegedly practicing such immorality. Although the investigation of the Denton in 1902 came to naught, hotels and boardinghouses would play a larger role in Springfield's prostitution in coming years.

At the start of the century, however, most of Springfield's painted ladies continued to ply their trade from their own residences or from houses belonging to madams. In August 1902, Cora Thomas, who lived in a room above a grocery store at the corner of Campbell and Walnut, complained to a grand jury that two young women who occupied a neighboring room above the store were using the room for immoral purposes. According to Cora, men came and went at all hours of the night. She further added that although both women were presently single, one of them had previously been married twice—a fact that Cora apparently thought might carry some weight with the jury. Her claims were substantiated by a man who lived in the same building with his family in a third apartment above the same store. The man reported overhearing conversations between the two young women and the men they brought to their room and had no doubt that they were using the place for prostitution.

In the fall of 1903, Harry Moran testified that he and Jim Couch had had sexual intercourse with two girls at Belle Watson's house at the northeast corner of Chase and Washington Streets in North Town. According to Moran, their friend Fred was still at the house when he and Couch left. Belle was charged a few months later with two counts of keeping a bawdyhouse. One charge was dropped, and she was acquitted of the other.

Like Belle Watson, Maud and Ruth Gibbs were frequently mentioned in connection to prostitution in Springfield during the early 1900s. The Gibbs girls, as they were usually called, were charged in 1903 with keeping a "house of ill favor" at the corner of Boonville and Water Streets. In 1905, Springfield chief of police J.R. McNutt told a grand jury that the girls had paid fines several times for renting rooms for immoral purposes. Kate Bird was another noted name in the Cyprian circles of Springfield in the early 1900s. Kate first showed up in court records in 1895 when she was charged with living in open adultery with John Moss at the corner of Water and Robberson Streets, but she had since moved on to more illicit activities. In 1903, she was charged with using her rooms near the corner of Olive Street and Patton Alley as a bawdyhouse. In the summer of 1907, Kate was busted for keeping a house of ill repute at the corner of Boonville Street and Phelps Avenue. She and her girls were ordered to report to the police court the next day, where they pled guilty and paid fines of $10.65 each. Some weeks later, an officer came around and wanted them to pay the same fine again without going to court, but they refused and complained to the police chief, who said he had not sent the officer. Kate thought the police harassment stemmed from the fact that the father of one of her girls was associated with the police department. At the same time Kate was keeping her house at Boonville Street and Phelps Avenue, she was also renting out her old rooms on Olive Street to sporting girls. Maude Scott and Annie Williams both testified that Kate knew they wanted the rooms for the purpose of having sexual intercourse with men when she rented them out.

Louis Price testified in 1905 that he knew the Jenkins Rooming House over a restaurant at 404 Commercial Street was being used as a bawdyhouse. He said he had seen boys between the ages of sixteen and eighteen "take girls in short dresses up to this rooming house." Price said that he voiced his concerns to the building's owner, F.D. Jenkins, but was told to keep his mouth shut. "I am going to make some money out of this business," Jenkins reportedly said.

Despite the increased competition, Martha Misner remained the undisputed queen of Springfield bawds in the early 1900s, as evidenced by her girls being repeatedly cited for prostitution between the years 1905 and 1908. Normally, the girls simply paid fines and were allowed to resume their vocation, but on occasion, a grand jury investigation resulted in them being brought to court.

In the summer of 1907, for instance, police raided the Plain View, charged Martha with keeping a bawdyhouse and called in her girls to testify against her. Cora Smith said that one time, while she was staying at Martha's place in December 1906, the police chief and two officers came and told her to report to police court. However, most of the time the girls paid fines directly to a police officer without arrests being made or formal charges being brought against them. Jennie Williams, Lena White, Maude Scott and Irene Sherman all testified that they had been fined in this manner while staying at the Plain View. Maude said that she had never been required to pay a fine except while she was staying with Martha, and she complained that the amount had recently gone up from $6.65 to $10.65. Irene added that Martha didn't help pay the fines and that, in order to compensate her for her loss of income, the girls had to pay the madam up to $2.50, depending on who the girl was, if they wanted to leave the house at night. By the time of their testimony in late August, Maude and Irene had already moved out of the Plain View.

Frankie Byrne, another of Mrs. Misner's girls, went into considerable detail about how the brothel operated. Not only did the girls have to pay Martha to leave at night, but they also paid her half of their earnings for room and board. "My income runs from $60 to $100 a week, and Martha Misner gets half and I get the other half," Frankie explained. "And I get my half every day." Frankie admitted that she had had sex with a man at the Plain View the day before her testimony. According to her, the price was set by Martha and collected by Rosa Cameron in "the presence of myself and the man whom I had intercourse with. I think the price was $3.00 with the man yesterday."

In 1908, when Martha Misner was again indicted for keeping a bawdyhouse, Frankie Byrne testified again and added more details about the operation. According to Frankie, Rosa would meet the man at the door of the Plain View and show him inside to the parlor. The girls were then called in and lined up in "plain view" so that the man could pick the one he wanted. Rosa agreed on a price with the man and collected the money (as the girls were "never allowed to collect the money"). At the end of each day, the girls were called into Martha's room and paid half of what Rosa had collected on their behalf. Frankie said she had made as much as $25.00 in a twenty-four-hour period. The Plain View was "considered a $1.00 house," but men had to pay $5.00 to stay all night. Frankie had apparently been with Martha long enough to become a "special" girl, which mean that she no longer had to pay to leave at night, even though the other girls still did. Cora Pittman echoed Frankie's testimony, although the most she had ever raked in at Martha Misner's was about $75.00 a week. She also named Lena Smith and Helen Hicks as two other girls who lived at the Plain View and added that Rosa Cameron "received company also." Madam Misner pled guilty in 1908 to the charge of keeping a bawdyhouse and paid a fine of $0.50 plus court costs. The fact that she had paid a $200.00 fine for the same offense the previous year illustrates how inconsistent authorities were in handling prostitution cases.

Although Martha Misner ran one of the few authentic bordellos (if not the only one) in Springfield during the early 1900s, freelance prostitutes plied their trade throughout the town, and by the latter half of the aughts, most of the self-employed girls worked out of hotels and boardinghouses rather than private residences. In the late summer of 1907, for instance, Della Reeve told a jury that for the past four weeks, she had been staying at 214½ North Jefferson with Irene Sherman, who had relocated from the Plain View. Before that, however, Della said she had stayed briefly at the Union Hotel, the Denton Hotel and the Central Hotel and that she had received men for the purpose of illicit intercourse at each place with the help of the hotel porters, who arranged the trysts. Sometimes the men came to her room, and sometimes she went to their rooms. She said she usually made about fifteen dollars a week from prostitution but sometimes could make as much as ten dollars a night.

After leaving Martha Misner's place about the same time as Irene Sherman, Maude Scott went to live on West Scott Street, where she occasionally entertained paying guests, but she spent most of her time making the rounds at the hotels, especially the Central Hotel at 505 Boonville Street. On Friday night, August 16, 1907, she paid fifty cents and checked in at the Central as Maude Scott from Kansas City, and the porter, who knew her to be a prostitute, took her to room no. 17. Shortly afterward, a man staying at the hotel asked the porter whether there was an available girl at the hotel, and the porter took her to Maude's room. The next morning, Maude paid the porter fifty cents for arranging the assignation. The next night, Saturday, the porter took Maude to two or three different men. However, two nights later, on Monday, August 19, Kate Bird came to the hotel asking to spend the night and was turned away. Apparently, even the Central Hotel had its standards.

Eva Keeling admitted to a grand jury in the summer of 1907 that she had been "following the sporting business" for about three years. She named several places in Springfield where she had plied her trade, including the Denton Hotel, and she said she normally made about ten or twelve dollars a day.

Clara Randall told a different grand jury in March 1908 that she had stayed at Galbreath's Rooming House at 321½ South Campbell Street for several months the previous year and received men there for the purpose of sexual intercourse. She said Galbreath not only knew about the assignations but also helped arrange them. Galbreath would charge the man one dollar for a room and then summon Clara to go to the man's room.

In early 1908, Clara moved to John Edwards's boardinghouse at 217½ North Campbell Street, where she and the other girls who stayed there had an understanding with Edwards that they were to receive men for the purpose of illicit intercourse. Clara paid three dollars a week for her room, and Edwards sometimes called her as many as two or three times a day to go to men's rooms. The visiting men paid one dollar each for their rooms, but according to Clara, they often only stayed for thirty minutes. Other working girls who either stayed at Edwards's place or used it as an assignation spot during Clara's time there included Anna Johnson, Ada Woods, Pearl Johnson, Leora Plummer, Marie Gillman and Florence Schurlock. The latter two girls later moved to a boardinghouse at 211½

West Walnut Street, where they had the same setup with the owner they had had at Edwards's place. Meanwhile, Maude Scott, who had left Mrs. Misner's Plain View Hotel to try to make it on her own, had moved again, this time from her Scott Street house to some rooms on the corner of Walnut and South Streets, where she was still entertaining men.

The judge's instructions to the March 1908 grand jury in Greene County suggests the prevalence of gambling and liquor violations in Springfield at the time. Speaking of the gambling laws, the judge cautioned, "At the outset, you can safely presume that these laws are constantly being violated. They always are." He warned the jurors of the many crimes begat by the pernicious gambling dens and suggested that "the alluring whispers of the professional gamblers" were often the downfall of young men who would not otherwise have dreamed of wrongdoing. The judge also wanted the jury especially to target drugstores that sold liquor illegally and saloons that sold to minors or on Sunday.

Although the judge did not include bawdyhouses and prostitution in issuing instructions to the grand jury, authorities did heavily crack down on the two near the end of 1908, especially after Chief Acie Loveless and the rest of the police department came under fire for their lax handling of "disorderly houses" and "dissolute women." According to the *Springfield Republican*, Loveless was determined "to follow up every opportunity to arrest those guilty of improper conduct," and sometime after December 1, Springfield police began a series of raids on the houses of ill repute. On the night of December 5, seven men and women were arrested for loitering at such places and required to put up a cash bond, pending their appearance in police court on Monday morning. Among those apprehended was Frankie Byrne, who had finally left Martha Misner and was now operating out of her own house.

In 1906, Mary Ferguson and her children occupied two rooms at 409 Boonville Street. Mary also oversaw several other rooms at the same location, two of which she rented to women of questionable character. When the two women were charged with and pled guilty to receiving men in their rooms for immoral purposes, Mary was also charged with "lodging in a bawdy house" and, according to her later testimony, told that she had to plead guilty, which she did. Even though there was no evidence that either Mary or her daughter was disreputable, Mary was later charged with keeping an underage girl, her fifteen-year-old

COMPLIMENTS OF
Lawson and Gibbs
WITH THE LAND TITLE COMPANY

Springfield square showing the Gottfried Tower, taken near the time the tower served as a scaffold for the lynching of three black men in 1906. *Courtesy Springfield–Greene County Library.*

daughter Leona, in a bawdyhouse, and she was convicted and sentenced to three years in prison. She appealed the conviction all the way to the Missouri Supreme Court, and it was overturned in 1909 on the grounds that, when she was convicted of keeping a girl in a bawdyhouse, the jury was not instructed to consider the question of whether she, indeed, *ran* a bawdyhouse. Rather, this fact was merely assumed based on her prior plea, even though there was almost no evidence to support it.

In addition to the vice and petty crimes chronicled in this chapter, a number of violent crimes also occurred during the first decade of the twentieth century. The most notorious was the 1906 lynching of three black men on the Springfield square, an event that made national headlines and has been featured in various history books. On Friday, April 13, a white woman who was estranged from her husband was out on the town with another man when the couple was stopped and the woman allegedly violated by two black men. Fred Coker and Horace Duncan were arrested and thrown in the county jail as suspects, even though evidence at the time seemed to exonerate them. On Saturday night, a mob formed, broke the pair out of the jail on North Robberson and marched them downtown. The procession halted at the Gottfried Tower, a metal structure several stories high that sat in the middle of the public square. The mob placed ropes around Coker's and Duncan's necks and tossed the other ends over the railing of the tower's bandstand, about twelve feet above the ground. The two men were then hoisted up in front of several thousand people. After the men were dead, their dangling bodies were doused with coal oil, and a fire was built beneath them. The flames licked upward, burning the ropes in two, and the corpses fell into the fire below, cremating them. The crowd then surged back to the jail and dragged out Will Allen, a young black man who was suspected of killing an older white man near Drury University a couple of months earlier. He, too, was taken back to the square, where he was mounted on the bandstand and given a mock trial. He was "convicted" in record time by the unruly throng and pushed over the railing with a rope around his neck. The rope gave way, and Allen fell into the burning pyre. He was pulled out and hanged a second time, but he was already dead by that point. His body was then tossed into the fire with the others. The next morning, citizens on their way to Easter Sunday services gawked at the smoldering ashes, and kids rummaged through them for souvenirs. Photographers took pictures of the gruesome scene to sell later, and one enterprising businessman even made medals commemorating the shocking event as the "Easter offering."

Chapter Nine

The Tameless Teens

By 1910, Springfield's population had grown to thirty-five thousand. Less isolated and parochial than it had once been, it was the hub of railway travel throughout southwest Missouri and beyond. With its awakening sophistication, however, came increased vice.

Prostitution, in particular, reached its zenith in Springfield during the 1910s. Continuing a trend that had begun the previous decade, most prostitutes opted for self-employment rather than working for a madam. Oftentimes, these working girls set up shop in hotels, many at the Denton Hotel on Campbell and College Streets. When hotel proprietor M.K. Watts learned a grand jury was set to convene in the fall of 1911, he told Lula Johnson and Nora Abbott, two young prostitutes who had been staying there for several weeks, to vacate the premises. The girls were called before the grand jury anyway, and Lula testified that she had frequently had paid sex with men at the Denton. According to her testimony, she registered under her own name and paid seventy-five cents a night for her room. The porter would take her to men's rooms, and she would sometimes entertain the men in their room or "sometimes I would take them to my own room." Nora added that she usually tipped the porter for soliciting the men for her. She said she made no effort to hide her business from Watts, and although they had not had any conversations about the subject, she felt sure he "was perfectly familiar with what was going on."

Watts and the black porter, Richard Burnett, were arrested and brought before the jury. Watts claimed he didn't know prostitutes were using the

Denton as a den of trade and was unaware that Burnett and some of the other porters were working the streets as pimps for their respective hotels. Burnett, on the other hand, denied that he had arranged any illicit trysts over the last twelve months. A witness who claimed that he himself had taken a woman to the Denton for immoral purposes told the jury that he considered the Denton "nothing but a bawdy house...conducted under the sign of a hotel." He went on to say that Burnett was usually paid 25 percent of what the working girls who stayed there made as his fee for hooking them up with men. Another man testified that Burnett had approached him several times near the Denton and proposed to get him a girl at the hotel if he would pay one dollar for the girl, fifty cents for the room and a quarter to Burnett. Watts was subsequently indicted for keeping a bawdyhouse while Burnett was charged with and convicted of perjury. Burnett appealed, but his conviction was upheld by the Missouri Supreme Court.

Despite its legal problems in late 1911, the Denton continued to be an assignation spot over the next few years. Seventeen-year-old Myrtle Weaver told a jury in November 1912 that she had left her home at Fair Grove several weeks earlier when she was still sixteen and made her way to Springfield, where M.K. Watts had employed her at the Denton for immoral purposes and had even occupied a room with her. She said that, on average, she was taken to four different men each night during the several days she stayed there. Less than a week after her arrival, Myrtle left the Denton when "she found out what kind of place it was."

W.W. Hendricks, who worked as a clerk at the Denton, testified that Watts had instructed him to charge the girls one dollar each for their rooms, while most guests paid only fifty or seventy-five cents. Watts, who was again indicted for keeping a bawdyhouse, had already left the Denton by late 1912, but prostitution continued at the hotel. In 1914, S.N. Warren named several girls, including Nell Bass and Dorothy Sims, as "hustlers" who stayed at or often visited the Denton.

Another favorite haunt of the ladies of the night was the Central Hotel at the corner of Boonville and Mill Streets. D.F. Yandle told a grand jury in the fall of 1911 that he had been employed there as a porter a few weeks earlier but was told he would not be paid a salary; instead, he would receive ten cents for each man he registered at the hotel and would make the rest of his money from the girls who stayed there by arranging "dates" for them with the men. The testimony of other Central Hotel porters mirrored that of D.F. Yandle.

During the same grand jury session, nineteen-year-old Bertha Townsend said she considered the Central a "safe place to go," because it was understood a girl could go there for immoral purposes and no questions would be asked. Eighteen-year-old Ruth White testified that she had gone to the Central for immoral purposes twice with Bertha and a few other times on her own. One night, Ruth had "sexual intercourse with various men" at a going rate of one dollar to two dollars "a bounce" and earned fifteen dollars that night, even after paying the porter twenty-five cents on each dollar she brought in. Alas, there were so many men, she declared, "that I cannot remember the number I stayed with." Another working girl, twenty-year-old Rose Cramer, said she would often register at the Central and then "scout around in the hall until I would meet a man, and we would go to his room, where we would have sexual intercourse." Minnie Smith, who stayed at the Central for about ten weeks prior to the middle of November, said that she and the four or five other girls who stayed there regularly had an understanding with the porters that they were "to give each one of us our turn," with no preference shown to one girl over another. Sometimes, these transient girls like Rose would "get out into the hall and hustle for themselves."

Following the investigation, Mr. and Mrs. Will Prevette, the Central Hotel's proprietors, were indicted for running a bawdyhouse, but the hotel continued its tacit operation as a bordello. Not long after Myrtle Weaver left the Denton in the fall of 1912, supposedly because she "found out what kind of place it was," she passed the Central Hotel, and a porter, aware of her reputation, invited her to come inside where he had procured two men looking for a good time. She accepted, and not long after, she was averaging "four different men each night." When the Prevettes were again charged with keeping a bawdyhouse, they followed the example of M.K. Watts at the Denton and turned ownership of the hotel over to someone else.

The Palace Hotel was the last of the "big three" Springfield hotels that prostitutes were known to frequent during the 1910s. The hotel, located at the corner of College and Market Streets, was originally erected in 1892 as the Eldridge Building. It became the Palace Hotel in 1908, and by the early part of the next decade, it was so busy that it opened three annexes (called rooming houses) nearby. Like the Denton and the Central, the Palace was within walking distance of the Gulf depot, now known as the Frisco depot, where porters often solicited hotel customers, especially those interested in extracurricular activities.

Photograph of the Palace Hotel. The hotel was one of Springfield's notorious assignation spots during the 1910s. *Photo by author.*

In the fall of 1912, J.W. Lloyd, an employee of the Palace, admitted to a grand jury that the hotel and its annexes "[were] all used for immoral purposes." The setup at the Palace was about the same as the Denton and Central in that the porters were paid little or nothing in wages but earned a living from the working girls to whom they brought clients. The porters not only hustled the streets and the area around the depot but also even staked out rival hotels on occasion. H.L. Maness, the proprietor of the nearby Ullman Hotel, complained that the porters from the Palace would stand in front of his hotel at College and Campbell Streets and try to lure his lodgers to the Palace with promises of pretty girls. Maness claimed Ferb Waddell and the other Palace porters were "experts at that kind of business."

Lena Sapp, a chambermaid at the Palace and niece of the proprietor, testified that she had no knowledge of immoral activities at the hotel, but her uncle, H.L. Malloch, was indicted nonetheless for running a bawdyhouse within one hundred yards of a church. Malloch was still running the Palace in 1915, and Ferb Waddell was still working as a porter there and making money by bringing girls clients. When called before a grand jury, Ferb testified that Malloch had recently told him to keep the girls away from the annexes because the police had them under close surveillance. Ferb named several of the girls, one of whom was Laura Kirk, who had been staying at the Palace. About a week earlier, Ferb had taken a man to Laura's room, but she refused, saying she did not want company. She also told Ferb that she had recently taken compound 606 (a treatment for syphilis discovered a few years earlier) and that because of her sickness, she had "not been receiving company as frequently as usual."

Although the hotels were home to most of the sporting action in the 1910s, the boardinghouses were still going strong as well. For instance, Minnie Smith, who stayed at the Central Hotel in late 1911, testified that she had previously rented a room at Mrs. Clemmons's boardinghouse at 222½ South Campbell Street, where she had made money for herself and the landlady by entertaining men. She left after Mrs. Clemmons got mad at her for taking off to attend a street fair in Ash Grove instead of staying at the house to make money. She and Mrs. Clemmons apparently reconciled though, because Minnie said that she had gone back to the boardinghouse with men several times since leaving the Central.

There were also still a few prostitutes who continued to use their private residences as bordellos. Frankie Byrne, who had previously worked for Martha Misner, ran a house near the intersection of Robberson and Pine Streets, where several other women had also set up shop in their homes. She was arrested in 1914 but, according to police records, was still in the business in 1916, entertaining men at the Leroy Rooms on West Walnut Street.

Some girls, such as Eunice McSlarrow, were gradually pressured into a life of prostitution. Sixteen-year-old Eunice came to Springfield in August 1912 from Mammoth Springs, Arkansas, at a time when many Springfield households, not just wealthy ones, had maids. Eunice spent three weeks as a hired girl at the Cox home, followed by a shorter stint with the Simons family. She then went to stay with the Brady family before going to work at the Royal Hotel. While at the Royal, she noticed several girls and women, including the female proprietor of the place, earning money by entertaining men, presumably a lot more money than she was making. Several men tried to get her to go to their rooms, but she refused and left the Royal after only four and a half days. She went to the Walnut Hotel on West Walnut Street and worked there a while before moving on to the Palace, where the porters began pressuring her to receive men for immoral purposes. She finally gave in and was soon entertaining men on a regular basis, sometimes "as many as 15 or 20 in a night." One time, she later recalled, she even got drunk and had sex with one of the black porters.

Some of the city's houses of assignation were granted special immunity from authorities and at a small price. Corruption in the ranks of Springfield's law enforcement, a recurrent but minor problem in previous decades, reached a head during the 1910s under the administration of Police Chief Thomas Hunter. Early on in his administration, Hunter instructed his policemen not to raid the immoral houses and gambling houses without his permission because he planned to handle them himself. He apparently had an ulterior motive for issuing such an order. Julia Quick told a grand jury in late 1911 that, while she was having sexual intercourse with a man at the Lindel Rooming House on a Saturday night the previous spring, Chief Hunter and the landlord interrupted them, and the landlord, after a conversation with Hunter, told her to meet the chief in his office the following Monday. She reported as told, and Hunter proposed to drop the charges against her and help her out in the future if she would meet him back at the Lindel that night. She again showed up as requested, and she and Hunter had sex in a room that the police chief had already reserved. During the same grand jury session, Pearl O'Toole, who ran the Vaughan Rooming House, testified that Chief Hunter tried on several occasions during the summer to intimidate her into paying fines for running a bawdyhouse even though she was running a legitimate boardinghouse. He finally arrested her, and according to Pearl, he grew angry and abusive in his language when she still denied the charge and told him that she was going to hire a lawyer.

Although the policemen were not authorized to raid bawdyhouses on their own, some of them apparently had prior knowledge of when such a raid was likely to occur. Minnie Smith told the jury that when she first came to the Central Hotel, she was worried about the place being raided, but the landlady told her that policemen Painter and Freeman would let them know when a raid was planned. Minnie said she later saw Painter and Freeman in bed with two girls in one of the rooms at the Central.

Not all city officials were in on the corruption, however. In late 1912, Julia Jenkins, who had taken over the Central Hotel after the Prevettes left, and partner Henry Hewitt devised a plan to trap city attorney Len Walker into meeting Effie Rowe, a prostitute, in a room at the Central and catch them in bed together. According to a third man who was in on the scheme, Hewitt wanted "to get hold of the son of a bitch [Walker]" and force him to stop the police raids. However, when Effie, who had been offered thirty-five dollars for her part in the scheme, approached Walker, he declined to go with her to the Central, and she ended up revealing the plan to him.

By 1914, the police protection that, two years earlier, had been secretly taken out in trade or purchased through systematic fines was openly sold to those who ran bawdyhouses. Julia Jenkins, who now ran the Oklahoma House, and her partner, Charles Hamel, told a grand jury that they usually paid $50 a month for police protection. "The things that went on after we got police protection," Julia said, "went on before we got police protection, but we were more careful about it." Still, there were some city officials who did not walk the path of corruption. Attorney Talma Hefferman said that he had been approached by Chief Hunter about making money off the houses of ill repute. "There are five or six big whorehouses in this town that need police protection," Hunter reportedly said. He speculated that the Denton and the Palace would each fetch $100 a month and proposed that authorities repeatedly raid the houses that refused to pay for protection, arrest the women working in them and then send the women to Hefferman with the advice that he could probably help them out. "In that way," he told the attorney, "you can make some good money." Hunter suggested a fifty-fifty split of the revenue, and he became very threatening and abusive when Hefferman balked at the proposition. Not long after, Chief Hunter was indicted on twelve counts of extortion and twelve counts of bribery, and the *Springfield Republican* published the following headline: "Police Station as a Center of Vice." Although Hunter was found not guilty on all counts, police corruption nonetheless declined after his legal difficulties.

Prostitution also tapered off in the late 1910s, and most of the red-light action that remained gravitated slightly westward, as many of the questionable resorts were clustered in the vicinity of Grant Avenue near its intersections with College and Olive Streets. Fannie Sutherland told a grand jury in 1919 that when she complained to Milt McClure about lewd women living in several houses he owned near Grant and Olive Streets, he told her that he minded his own business and for her to do the same. When Mrs. A.L. McQuisten lodged a similar complaint, McClure told her that if the old women in the neighborhood didn't keep their mouths shut, he would rent his houses to blacks. Another neighbor,

Phoebe Evans, testified that it was "unsafe for a lady to go along College Street at night," and Fred Walker said he had been accosted several times by women near Grant and Olive Streets and told that, for three dollars, he could stay all night with them. Walker said his wife had also been bothered by the women, and the couple finally moved out of the neighborhood to get away from the loose women.

Gambling continued to flourish in the 1910s. During a crackdown on the gaming houses in the summer of 1910, Springfield police conducted three raids and caught almost fifty men playing poker. Although Ed Drew's upstairs room at the corner of Boonville Street and Phelps Avenue was still hopping during the 1910s, it was likely not one of the places authorities raided. Sometime after the 1906 lynchings, the club became strictly a club for blacks and, according to one officer, was rarely raided, even though it operated all hours of the day. Another popular gambling spot during the 1910s was a room over Hurlburt and McCoy's billiard hall on College Street. In the fall of 1911, Jerome Stutzman was busted for running a nickel-quarter poker game there.

Sometime around June 1, 1912, the City of Springfield passed an ordinance legalizing slot machines to be used strictly for entertainment purposes, and sixteen licenses to house the machines were given out to businesses throughout town. The law, however, was rescinded less than a month later when officials realized that many of the machines were being used as gambling devices.

Liquor violations were common in Springfield during the 1910s as they had been in years past. Saloons were sometimes busted for staying open on Sunday, and druggists and other merchants were still occasionally charged with selling liquor without a license. However, the real point of emphasis in enforcement of liquor laws was trying to stem the tide of alcohol sales to minors. During crackdowns, teenager after teenager caught in possession of beer or liquor was dragged before a grand jury and compelled to tell where he had gotten it. In December 1911, eighteen-year-old James Stemmons testified that he had bought and drunk beer at the Blue Ribbon Bar in the Kirby Arcade, Rose's saloon on Boonville Street, McGarvey's place on Boonville Street and Kelly and Kerr's saloon on College Street. The following year, sixteen-year-old Smith Brown said he had bought whiskey at the Metropolitan Hotel bar, the Kentucky Liquor House and the Green Light Saloon, among several other places.

Cartoon from the *Springfield Missouri Republican* printed on the eve of Prohibition.

Temperance crusaders, who had been trying to make the sale of liquor illegal in Springfield and elsewhere throughout the country for many years, finally saw their efforts come to fruition with passage of the Volstead Act in 1919. Most of the provisions of the Prohibition law took effect on July 1, 1919, and the previous day, many people in Springfield rushed to stock up for what the *Springfield Leader* called the "big dry spell." The *Leader* went on to describe the festivities as a send-off: "On what promises to be the last day of his life, John Barleycorn was the kingpin at many little farewell parties today in Springfield. The saloons and wholesale liquor houses were crowded with persons from the city and adjoining counties and all dealers were employing a double force of help." But alcohol did not go out with a bang as much as a whimper. There were no reports in the town dailies the next day of carousing or drunken mêlées in the streets. Springfield's eighty-year, love-hate relationship with alcohol was now on hold.

Epilogue

I chose the beginning of the Prohibition era as a stopping point for this book because there was a noticeable drop-off in vice as a whole after 1919. Crime obviously picked up later on and, in some cases, was fueled by Prohibition. There were a number of notorious incidents in Springfield's history that I could have included, notably the Young brothers' massacre of law officers just west of town in 1932. However, this work was intended to be a brief history of Springfield, so I chose to concentrate only on its early years.

Bibliography

Books and Magazine Articles

Escott, George S. *History and Directory of Springfield and North Springfield.* Springfield, MO: *Patriot-Advertiser*, 1878.

Fairbanks, Jonathan, and Clyde Edwin Tuck. *Past and Present of Greene County, Missouri.* Indianapolis, IN: A.W. Bowen, 1915.

The Graham Tragedy and the Molloy-Lee Examination: The Only Authentic History of the Murder of Sarah Graham, by Her Husband, George E. Graham, Near Springfield, Missouri, on the Night of September 30, 1885. 1886. Reprint, Springfield, MO: Greene County Archives and Records Center, 2001.

Holcombe, R.I., ed. *History of Greene County, Missouri.* 1883. Reprint, Clinton, MO: The Printery, 1969.

Hubble, Martin J. *Personal Reminiscences and Fragments of the Early History of Springfield, Greene County, Missouri.* Springfield, MO: Inland Printing Company, 1914.

An Illustrated Historical Atlas Map of Greene County, MO. N.p.: Brink, McDonough, 1876.

Langsdorf, Edgar. "Letters of Joseph H. Trego, 1857–1864, Part 2." *Kansas Historical Quarterly* 19 (August 1951).

Laws Applicable to and Governing the City of Springfield, Greene County, Missouri. Springfield, MO: D.C. Young, 1897.

Pickrell, Martha M. *Emma Speaks Out: Life and Writings of Emma Molloy (1839–1907).* Carmel, IN: Guild Press, 1999.

Pictorial and Genealogical Record of Greene County, Missouri. Chicago: Goodspeed Publishing, 1893.

Reports of Cases Determined in the Supreme Court of the State of Missouri Between May 31 and July 1, 1909. Vol. 221. Columbia, MO: E.W. Stephens, 1909.

Rosa, Joseph G. "'Little Dave's' Last Fight: What Really Happened When Wild Bill Hickok and Davis K. Tutt Shot It Out at Springfield, Missouri." *Quarterly of the National Association for Outlaw and Lawman History* 20, no. 4 (October–December 1996).

———. *They Called Him Wild Bill.* Norman: University of Oklahoma Press, 1964.

Southwestern Reporter. Vol. 161. St. Paul, MO: West Publishing, 1914.

Springfield City Directories, various years.

GOVERNMENT DOCUMENTS AND UNPUBLISHED MANUSCRIPTS

Gates, Staci L. "Prostitution in Springfield: From Quiet Tolerance to Progressive Reform, 1861–1914." Seminar paper submitted to the Department of History, Southwest Missouri State University, Springfield, Missouri, 2004.

Greene County Circuit Court Records.

Greene County Coroner's Record Books.

Greene County Court Records.

Greene County Grand Jury Books.

Greene County Marriage Records.

Phelps County Circuit Court Records.

U.S. Bureau of the Census.

U.S. Provost Marshals' Papers. Individual Citizens Files. Missouri State Archives. Jefferson City, Missouri.

U.S. Provost Marshals' Papers. Two or More Citizens Files. Missouri State Archives. Jefferson City, Missouri.

ONLINE SOURCES

Community and Conflict: The Impact of the Civil War in the Ozarks. www.ozarkscivilwar.org.

The History of the Mercer County Sheriff's Office online. ww.grm. net/~mercoso/MCSO/History.html.

Moon City Press webpage. www.mooncitypress.com.

NEWSPAPERS

Columbia Missouri Statesman
Joplin Daily Herald
Liberty (MO) Tribune
New York Times
Springfield Advertiser
Springfield Daily Herald
Springfield Express
Springfield Leader
Springfield Leader Democrat
Springfield Mirror
Springfield Missouri Republican
Springfield Missouri Weekly Patriot
Springfield News-Leader
Springfield Patriot Advertiser
Springfield Republican
Springfield Times
Springfield Weekly Patriot

Index

About the Author

Larry Wood is a retired public school teacher and a freelance writer. His historical articles have appeared in numerous publications, including *America's Civil War*, *Blue and Gray*, *Gateway Heritage*, *Missouri Life*, *Missouri Historical Review*, the *Ozarks Mountaineer*, *True West* and *Wild West*. His titles *Civil War Springfield*, *The Two Civil War Battles of Newtonia* and *Wicked Joplin* are available from The History Press. A native of Fair Grove, Missouri, Wood received his BA and MA degrees from Missouri State University and now lives in Joplin with his wife, Gigi.

Visit us at
www.historypress.net